Battle Creek

PRODUCED IN COOPERATION WITH THE
BATTLE CREEK AREA
CHAMBER OF COMMERCE

WINDSOR PUBLICATIONS, INC.
WOODLAND HILLS, CALIFORNIA

Battle Creek

THE PLACE BEHIND THE PRODUCTS

AN ILLUSTRATED HISTORY

BY LARRY B. MASSIE & PETER J. SCHMITT

*For Ross H. Coller and Berenice Lowe,
whose lives were well spent tracing the
history of Battle Creek.*

Windsor Publications
History Books Division
Publisher: John M. Phillips
Editorial Director, Corporate Biographies: Karen Story
Assistant Director, Corporate Biographies: Phyllis Gray
Senior Picture Editor: Teri Davis Greenberg
Marketing Director: Ellen Kettenbeil
Design Director: Alexander D'Anca
Production Manager: Dee Cooper
Typesetting Manager: E. Beryl Myers
Proofreading Manager: Doris R. Malkin

Staff for *Battle Creek: The Place Behind the Products*
Editor: Annette Igra
Picture Editor: Julie Jaskol
Corporate Biographies Editor: Judith Hunter
Editorial Assistants: Kathy Brown, Patricia Buzard, Ethel
  Karcz, Gladys McKnight, Lonnie Pham, Pat Pittman
Sales Manager: Bob Moffitt
Sales Representatives: Chuck Saxon, Cal Young
Layout Artist: Chris McKibbin
Proofreaders: Lynn Johnson, Jeff Leckrone
Typographers: Barbara Neiman, Cynthia Pinter

Designer: Alexander D'Anca

Library of Congress Cataloguing in Publication Data

Massie, Larry B., 1947-
  Battle Creek, the place behind the products.

  "Produced in cooperation with the Battle Creek
Area Chamber of Commerce."
  Bibliography: p. 128
  Includes index.
  1. Battle Creek (Mich.)—History. 2. Battle Creek
(Mich.)—Description. 3. Battle Creek (Mich.)—
Industries. I. Schmitt, Peter J. II. Battle Creek
Area Chamber of Commerce. III. Title.
F574.B2M37 1984   977.4'22   84-15247

ISBN 0-89781-117-8

Preceding page: *Peaceful Battle Creek, once a source of power for early industry, still winds through the heart of downtown. Courtesy, Peter J. Schmitt*

Contents

The sweetheart of the corn

Kellogg's
TOASTED CORN FLAKES

Made from the sweet hearts of the best white corn, skillfully cooked, flaked and toasted — giving it the flavor that won immediate favor. The great factory at Battle Creek works night and day to supply the ever-increasing demand for this delicious food. If you've never tried Kellogg's get a package today. Just tell your grocer you want the genuine — that nothing else will do.

THE ORIGINAL HAS THIS SIGNATURE

W. K. Kellogg

Introduction

From "The Sweetheart of the Corn" to "Tony the Tiger," generations of youngsters sent envelopes bulging with box tops to Battle Creek—"the Cereal City" and one of America's best-known place names. Over the years not only cereals but a host of other products ranging from threshing machines to violin strings have carried the name around the world.

There is no other place quite like Battle Creek. But Battle Creek's history, as it developed from frontier settlement to bustling railroad town to urban and industrial center, is the story of America itself. In the 1830s and 1840s, pioneer families pushed beyond the roadways to settle on Goguac Prairie or on the area's many "oak openings." Early settlers built their first homes of logs, and many lived with dirt floors and ax-hewn furniture. Like all frontier folks, they hunted and fished and swapped with their neighbors while waiting for their first crops. They wrote to far-off friends and hoped for health and good harvests. The county's few doctors and preachers traveled from cabin to cabin, sometimes blazing their own trails, so poor were early roads. A broken plowshare or an empty flour barrel meant a long trip to the nearest trading center. Local settlers welcomed the first tavern and store in Battle Creek, and the millrace Sands McCamly dug in 1835 brought hope to all the neighborhood.

Battle Creek grew rapidly in the frontier years. Its location at the junction of the creek and the Kalamazoo River brought investors interested in waterpower for mills and factories. The Michigan Central Railroad, coming in 1845, brought markets closer and cut travel time from weeks to hours.

Other towns along the river and the railroad shared these advantages, and many prospered. Jackson and Albion to the east and Kalamazoo to the west showed similar patterns. But not every town seemed equally successful. Marshall, the county seat for Calhoun County, became the largest town in the pioneer period. Optimists predicted it might even become the state capital. But Marshall's population peaked in the 1870s and then began a slow decline. By 1910 half the people in the county lived in Battle Creek.

Several factors influenced Battle Creek's success. First was the ingenuity of its entrepreneurs. One after another, early businessmen developed imaginative products to meet the needs of an ever-widening market. As times changed, these entrepreneurs and others like them found new products or attracted new industries to fill the buildings vacated by failure.

Particularly after the Civil War, the growth of local industry seemed little short of phenomenal. New firms came, attracted by success, and others grew vigorously. Most of these early industries followed predictable patterns as they developed finished products from local raw materials. Battle Creek's early preeminence as a flour-milling center, its woolen mills, and Willard Jeft's extension table factory provide examples.

At a time when farming still dominated the national economy, industrialists responded with products that revolutionized agriculture. Implement makers in Jackson, Albion, Battle Creek, and Kalamazoo found ready markets. Local businessmen made fortunes building better plows, harrows, or threshing machines. Ingenious mechanics found ready opportunities to design new and better products. Local schoolboy Constantius Case went to work in the Nichols & Shepard thresher works long enough to see what improvements he could make, then he founded the Advance Threshing Machine Company in competition. Others did likewise.

Battle Creek owed its success to no single key, but investment capital played an important role. Well-to-do farmers and merchants had money to invest in the 1870s and 1880s. Early industrialists put their profits into new enterprises. Key businessmen held offices in several companies at the same time, to protect their investments or to capitalize on their own management skills.

By the turn of the century, people around the country knew Battle Creek and its products. Its factories numbered more than a hundred, of which cereal companies were but one segment. Tall buildings punctuated the skyline, and business boomed. The town continued to grow under the watchful eyes of Edwin Nichols, Charles W. Post, Will K. Kellogg, and other successful businessmen.

Battle Creek also mirrored America's social movements. A variety of religious and social

Facing page: The Sweetheart of the Corn® appeared as a contemporaneously attractive country lass in 1911. The sweetheart evolved during the following decades to mirror changing ideals of bucolic beauty. Copyright, 1984, courtesy, Kellogg Company

experiments flourished in western New York in the 1820s and 1830s. Emigrants from the Empire State brought many unconventional beliefs to Battle Creek—already known as a liberal haven. In the 1850s James and Ellen White arrived to make Battle Creek the headquarters for Seventh-Day Adventism—a new offshoot of the "Millerite" excitement in the East. That event influenced the subsequent economic development of the whole area. Soon the Seventh-Day Adventist press began sending millions of tracts throughout the world. For the remainder of the century, books bearing Battle Creek imprints advised the nation on health reform, vegetarianism, massage, and "hydropathy," while the church's Health Reform Institute demonstrated these techniques.

In the 1870s John Harvey Kellogg renamed the Institute "Battle Creek Sanitarium." Soon "the San" became a mecca for the run-down rich and famous who sought rejuvenation through Dr. Kellogg's gospel of fresh air and sunshine combined with enemas, "nuttolene," and "protose." John Harvey Kellogg, a five-foot, three-inch dynamo, authored scores of books popularizing his eccentric theories, and in his spare time invented peanut butter, granola, and cornflakes as health foods.

But it took the advertising genius of Charles W. Post to make Battle Creek the nation's "breakfast food capital." Following a stay at "the San" in the 1890s, Post started his own mystical health institute, "La Vita Inn," and began to market breakfast foods. America's enthusiasm for "Postum," "Post Toasties," and "Grape Nuts" made him a millionaire. His success inspired the breakfast food boom of 1902. Local entrepreneurs organized more than 80 cereal companies, including "Malta-Vita," "Cereola," "Flak-Oata," "Egg-O-See," "Sanitary My-O," and "Frumenta" (a flake with painfully sharp cutting edges). Few of these companies survived, but one that outdistanced its competitors was run by W.K. Kellogg. He autographed his own products with a Spencerian flourish—"None Genuine Without This Signature"—and made his handwriting the most widely reproduced in history.

Battle Creek development suggests what many communities experienced as they grew from frontier village to farming town and factory city. Invention and canny investment along with management skill and a fair amount of luck boomed the city into the modern world. It is hard to tell such a complex story in any way more orderly than the experience itself. A simple chronicle of a city in transition keeps the facts in order, but we understand the forces at work only by a fuller treatment of special experiences. Thus, Chapter I deals with the pioneer era, covering little more than a decade in the 1830s and 1840s. Chapter II details the establishment of an economy based on manufacturing. In the next half-century Battle Creek became a city and built an industrial work place.

Larry Massie's Chapters III, IV, and V explore the impact of urbanization and industrialization in three key areas. Battle Creek's fame spread across the country through its publishing industry, its health facilities, and, in the 20th century, its preeminence as the world's "cereal capital." Important as these developments proved to be, however, Battle Creek continued to display the economic and social concerns common to other modern communities. Chapter VI treats the city's adjustments to 20th-century living, covering the impact of Fort Custer, the Depression, and the boom years after World War II.

Sands McCamly first platted Battle Creek close to waterpower and transportation routes. Later highways and railroads proved him right. But the city's success was more than an accident of good location, and more than simple economic forces. People made the difference. Flamboyant personalities made their mark on Battle Creek's history. Outspoken human rights advocate Sojourner Truth was widely known, and hundreds of thousands followed Ellen White's visions. Less famous but equally colorful were James Peebles, "spiritual pilgrim" and quack healer, Bernarr Macfadden, America's prototype stong man, the Lambert family and their manuals of "Nut Cookery," Mrs. M.E. Pendill, "The Celebrated Indian Doctress," and Mrs. Ellen Overholt with her electrical baths. Nevertheless, Sands McCamly's first vision of a thriving manufacturing center depended on unsung laborers fashioning their products with now-forgotten skills. Schoolteacher Anson Van Buren, candy-maker Alex Ratti, mayor Frederick Brydges, or any of a hundred others like them helped make Battle Creek what it is today. To some extent, this book is their story.

CHAPTER I

Alone in the Woods

Edward Tiffin was no fool. He'd been governor of Ohio and now was Surveyor General of the Northwest. He sat making out his report and hoping the President would intervene to stop what seemed to him a fruitless search. It was 1815, and Congress offered veterans of the War of 1812 six million acres of "bounty lands" in the West. Tiffin was charged with finding two million acres of potential farmland in Michigan Territory, but his surveyors argued it was hopeless. They agreed that not one percent of the proposed land could ever be farmed. He asked "to pay off what has been done and abandon the country." Then he added his own description of southern Michigan:

the country is, with some few exceptions, low wet land with a very thick growth of underbrush, intermixed with very bad marshes. . . . the number and extent of swamps increase with the addition of a number of lakes from 20 chains to two and three miles across. . . . The intermediate space between these swamps and lakes, which is probably near one-half the country, is, with a very few exceptions, a poor, barren, sandy land on which scarcely any vegetation grows except very small scrubby oaks. In many places that part which may be called dry land is composed of little short of sand hills forming a kind of deep basin, the bottom of many of which are composed of a marsh similar to those above described. The streams are generally narrow and very deep compared with their width, the shores and bottoms of which are with a very few exceptions swampy beyond description and it is with difficulty that a place can be found over which horses can be conveyed.

Emigrants poured into the Ohio Valley and spread across the Old Northwest; but they bypassed Michigan Territory for lands further south in Ohio, Indiana, and Illinois. In part they followed the great river highways of the Ohio Valley; but in part they believed school-book stories of Michigan's "interminable swamps." Governor Lewis Cass did what he could to promote the territory and arranged for a government land office in Detroit, but years passed before surveyors finally worked their way across the southern two tiers of counties in the late 1820s. Only then did reports of dry ground, oak openings, and tallgrass prairies

filter eastward.

Calhoun County had its streams and marshes, but it also offered more than a third of a million acres of level or gently rolling land. This land was rich and ready for the plow on Goguac and Dry prairies and on parklike openings elsewhere. Virgin hardwoods rose majestically along the river bottoms, including the soft tulip poplar or "whitewood" so prized for building. Occasional hay marshes indicated wet ground but also good forage for livestock. Marshall sandstone outcroppings in several townships provided easy building stone. In 1877 one pioneer historian recalled that game was everywhere. There were deer, bear, and wolves; skunks "perfumed every breeze;" prairie chickens boomed; "partridges drummed on every log;" turkeys strutted in the openings; "wild ducks literally blackened the streams and ponds;" and pigeons "darkened the sun." Streams fell steeply into the Kalamazoo River valley to provide waterpower sites for early industry. Early maps gave "Battle Creek" a prominent place in the northwest part of the county. Two government surveyors who camped on this stream drew blood in a brawling exchange with two Potawatomies. The surveying party retreated to Detroit and awaited Governor Cass' peacemaking before finishing their work and naming the stream. They found Calhoun County one of the most attractive areas in the state, as Potawatomies in the area's several villages had always known.

The Erie Canal opened in 1825, and its color-ful canalboats carried emigrants from the Northeast quickly and cheaply to the West. These emigrants boarded steamboats to cross Lake Erie. The *Walk-On-Water* made its first trip from Buffalo to Detroit in 1818. When the canal opened, six steamboats served the lake ports. Ten years later, 90 of them splashed back and forth to Detroit, which replaced Pittsburgh as the staging area for western travel.

Detroit in the late 1820s straggled along the riverbank, home to scarcely 3,000 people. Wagons passing and repassing churned the dirt streets into mud or raised clouds of dust as emigrants organized for the final leg of their westward travel. Old and new friends shouted goodbyes as some headed north toward Pontiac and others southwest. Still others struck west towards Ypsilanti and the "Territorial Road," which the legislature authorized in 1829. In 1831 O.G. Steele's "New and Correct Map of Michigan" showed it stretching west, an unbroken ribbon through Washtenaw, Jackson, and Calhoun counties.

Landlookers carrying this new map could travel through Ann Arbor, founded in 1824, and "Jacksonburgh," only a few weeks old but already on the map. They would note that the road continued west without a single settlement; the map marked only the gridiron survey of numbered townships and counties bravely named after President Andrew Jackson and his cabinet. The older Chicago Military Road to the south carried the dignified name of "Turnpike," but no one had improved either

Above: *The Kalamazoo River linked the major communities in Calhoun County. This circa 1910 view is from the western edge of Battle Creek. Courtesy, Michigan Room, Willard Public Library*

Facing page: *Volunteers dismantled this pioneer log cabin and reassembled it in Leila Arboretum as part of the city's Sesquicentennial celebration in 1981. Courtesy, Peter J. Schmitt*

road beyond Ann Arbor. Surveyors followed Indian trails, blazing trees with "H" for "highway" along the Territorial Road. As far as the map extended, the streams were unbridged, the marshes unfilled, and the hills ungraded.

Heavy freight wagons devastated the Indian footpaths. Each traveler tried his best to find a way that would avoid the deepest ruts and mistaken routes of his predecessors. Alone or in small parties, early settlers averaged a mile and a half an hour in good going and sometimes little more than that from dawn to dark. One settler wryly described a "Michigan mile" as crossing one section and circling two. Mistakes could be costly. A mired wagon might require a half-dozen oxen or more to pull it free. A broken axle meant disaster far from repairs. One newspaper account in 1836 said the road looked like "the route of a retreating army, so great is the number of different kinds of wrecks which it exhibits." Anson Van Buren agreed that "the bottom had fallen out," adding "the *bad* in the road had a deeper meaning than in any road we ever saw before." Time after time his wagon mired in the ruts of those who had gone before, and the whole party waited for help from those who came after. In such ways

emigrants formed friendships that sometimes lasted a lifetime. Writing almost 40 years later, Van Buren remembered:

We found scattered along the road here and there poles and rails, used as levers, broken tongues, pieces of felloes, an old wagon wheel, or an entire old wagon, and sometimes an old abandoned stage coach lay careened and moldering by the road side, each fragment or hulk telling a tale of adventure or mishap—mute reminders of the trials of those emigrants who had gone before. There was no chance to repair; whatever broke or gave out must be used as long as it could be, and then was abandoned.

However bad the going, emigrants hoped to make their way to a log tavern or a settler's home by nightfall. However, there were inns every few miles east of Jackson, and every settler "kept tavern;" passing emigrants were among the few who still had ready cash for a bite to eat and a place on the floor.

They were not ordinary travelers who looked at early maps and struck out for the frontier. Young or old, rich or poor, they moved across the land with single-minded purpose. To reach their new homes they surmounted obstacles, because they had no other choice. As Anson Van Buren put it, "they had to find a way to travel or make one." Some were wealthy and came to pioneering "full-handed." Such was Englishman John Bertram, who entered more than 1,500 acres in Emmett and Marshall townships and paid cash for all he needed, yet still had $10,000 at interest in Detroit. Others, like 16-year-old Caroline Sharpsteen and her husband, came because land was cheap. Still others hoped to build a patrimony for their children. Isaac Thomas established a family colony on Goguac Prairie in 1831 with his four married sons and assorted friends and relatives. He moved on to Illinois in 1839, searching for still cheaper and more spacious land for his heirs. John D. Pierce and his young wife represented the American Home Missionary Society in 1831. One traveler caught up to them in the rain-soaked darkness outside Marshall, singing hymns to keep up their spirits as their open wagon lurched slowly through the mud. They preached the first sermon in Marshall to 25 people in an unfinished, dirt-floored shanty. Anson Van Buren was 14 and George Willard

12 when they came with their parents in the early 1830s. Lankford Burdick's four-year-old daughter said of her trip to Charleston, "there was a great deal of water and no bridges, a great farm with no fences [the prairie land] and one hundred and two mudholes."

Each pioneer faced the last goodbyes at home with mixed emotions. Philena Ainsley heard a sermon on the way and waited a year before she heard another. Anson Van Buren listened to his first train whistle as he left his New York home. He would wait 10 years to hear another. George Willard and his family traveled from Vermont to Detroit in two weeks, then spent another two weeks from Detroit to Battle Creek in 1836. Pioneers remembered the trip from Detroit for the rest of their lives. For many it was their last great adventure.

In 1850 Philena Ainsley wrote of her own trip. She and her husband, John, sold everything but a salt dish and some bedclothes. They left Pennsylvania on June 3, 1831, carrying two trunks, a chest of carpenter's tools, and a 10-month-old daughter. They had $300 for land and supplies. Two weeks later they reached Detroit wondering where to turn. J.J. Guernsey advised them to head for Battle Creek. He himself had just entered his claim to land there at the government land office. A friendly traveler agreed to carry their trunks, and Mrs. Ainsley when the going was good. The party reached Ann Arbor after two hot, muddy days. Mrs. Ainsley remembered walking five miles at a stretch carrying her fussing baby. West of Ann Arbor, the Ainsleys rented part of a one-room log cabin while John went on to locate land. His wife shared quarters with two other families—19 people in all and a single bed. Toward the end of July the Ainsleys hired a man with a breaking plow to carry them to Marengo Township and to turn over prairie sod for their first crops.

With only three houses between Jacksonburgh and Marengo, the Ainsleys made their way alone. Their last night out they came upon an Indian encampment with "dogs and guns, papooses and ponies, strewn over the ground in every direction." A short distance further they found Squire Neal's—"the first and only house at that time in Marengo." Next morning they trekked the last two miles to a new home "with the sky above and the earth beneath."

The Ainsleys, like most pioneers, spent their first hectic days arranging for shelter and survival. A bedsheet over the bushes sheltered them for three weeks while John worked on a simple cabin. Rain fell nearly every day, but their furniture was waterproof, and a washtub covered the baby. On August 25, 1831, they moved into their cabin with a shingled roof and dirt floor. Few settlers had carpenter's tools, so young John began to "finish" his neighbors' homes, hewing the first puncheon floors in the county.

With a flour barrel for a cupboard, a chest for a table, and two trunks for seats, the Ainsleys were as well furnished as most settlers. They built their bed of poles and wagon boards, and Mrs. Ainsley complained that it looked "as though an Elephant had stepped on it." Since there was no wheat, there could be no straw for the bed tick. The Ainsleys used oak leaves at first, then marsh hay unil next year's harvest.

With the flour barrel nearly empty, John traveled 50 miles to the nearest mill and was 11 days returning. By midwinter the cupboard held nothing but salt, pepper, and cranberries supplied by neighboring Indians. John took his oxen and sleigh some 65 miles to Ann Arbor, the nearest market town. On his return one ox died, and he yoked himself with the other for the last three miles. By spring the family had sold their wagon, sleigh, ox, and rifle. But they owned their cabin and 160 acres of land. John made a cart for drawing fence rails that he and his wife could move "by both pulling one way, which all married couples should do." That summer they fenced 20 acres to wheat and to potatoes obtained from Titus Bronson, five days westward. Their future seemed secure as they watched their own fields expanding and new

Early steamboats carried new settlers across Lake Erie, as shown in this engraving called a "tradesman's cut." These illustrations were available through printer's catalogs, and were used in ads in newspapers throughout Michigan in the mid-19th century. Courtesy, Western Michigan University Archives

This Native American warrior once stood in McCamly Park. It was moved to Irving Park, which opened in 1924 and boasted a pond, brook, woods, and plants imported from all over the country. Courtesy, Peter J. Schmitt

neighbors coming each season.

By 1836 Anson Van Buren and his family found thrifty pioneer farms like the Ainsleys' on every hand. The Territorial Road ran through frontier Battle Creek, along present-day Marshall Street and Virginia Avenue, across the river at a shallow point, and on out Territorial Avenue. The Van Burens passed a dozen pioneer cabins as they traveled west that last October day. Eventually they crossed through a timbered area and onto their own land. "We were alone in the silent woods," said young Van Buren, and far from neighbors. Only their faces and their furniture reminded them of the home they had left. Even familiar birds and insects, rats and mice were absent in the wilderness. Mrs. Olive Van Buren wept with homesickness a year later when she found a housefly pressed in a family book. But now there was much to do before the family faced their first Michigan winter. There was game to be hunted in the woods and marsh hay to be cut for the stock. There could be little time for feeling lonely.

Like so many settlers, the Van Burens spent their money on land and cabin and had only their labor left for capital. As latecomers to Goguac, their labor was much in demand. Husking corn, digging potatoes, and helping slaughter earned payment in kind. Some things were unavailable for any amount of money. Wheat and corn could be had, but the nearest gristmill was 17 miles away—a two- or three-day trip by ox team. Pork and beef were scarce enough. Oxen were too useful to slaughter, and the Van Burens' first pig, fattened on acorns, "was so lean it would not fry itself." Five hundred pounds of dried codfish brought from home against emergencies provided welcome relief and stock for trading with neighbors. Van Buren wrote many years later that "everybody borrowed and everybody lent" in those early days when "undergoing common hardships made friends and equals of all."

"The first settlers of the wilderness have a peculiar experience which the country once occupied and improved can never afford," E.G. Rust said in his 1869 history of Calhoun County. He found pioneers in every township who remembered the early days. "Hundreds," he wrote, "look back on those times with the most

inexpressible delight." Neighborhoods seemed united then, and people of every social class seemed on equal footing. Time softened hardships as one pioneer after another recalled "making land." Whatever their origins, they faced common needs for shelter, cropland, and social contacts.

Wherever they located, the first settlers needed homes. If they came in springtime when the sap was running, they could strip off long rolls of tree bark for temporary shanties. Later arrivals might use bundles of marsh hay for thatch. Lumber and bricks were unavailable. All across the county first settlers chopped and sawed and pulled green logs for building. Some labored alone or with their families. Others asked for help. In return for a barrel of whiskey or homemade beer, neighbors came from miles around for a day-long "raising." Everyone turned out willingly, because each might have to ask for help in return. Anson Van Buren remembered, "at that early day people who lived twenty miles apart, lived nearer together than many people do now who live in sight of each other."

With a man at each corner to notch the logs and a crew to raise them into position, the pioneer cabin was all in a day's work. Eighteen by 20 feet or 20 by 26 feet, as available timber might dictate, these first cabins were primitive affairs—often a single room with a sleeping loft above, dirt-floored and barely lit through one or two windows. Moss and mud kept out the wind and snow when tightly packed between the logs, but hand-split shakes quickly weathered and often leaked. Philena Ainsley remembered, "we had little room and needed less," and even the wealthiest settlers were scarcely better off. Mrs. Chloe Dryer said her family hauled lumber for miles to build a real "frame" shanty. The green boards soon warped in the summer sun, and the family was happy enough to build again of logs.

George Ketchum wrote in April 1831 that he had traveled four-and-a-half days from Ann Arbor to Marshall with two wagons, four oxen, seven men, and one woman. He and his men began building the first cabin at Marshall, but no sooner were the bottom logs in place than driving rain forced the laborers under temporary shelters of peeled bark. "We were a sorry-looking set, all smoke and wet," he wrote,

These early color prints of Battle Creek show Monument Square and its leisurely strolling inhabitants in the first decades of the 20th century. Courtesy, Michigan Room, Willard Public Library

adding, "it rained so hard we could cook nothing, and we began to think it was hard times in Michigan." Still, the sun shone next day, and 48 hours later he and his men had raised a one-and-a-half story, 20-by-26-foot log home, partly chinked with the rafters up.

Stephen Eldred settled a few miles west of Battle Creek in 1831. He built a sawmill his first summer and planned in 1833 to raise the largest barn in the area. He pulled his timber to the site, killed a beef, and brewed a kettle of beer. Then he called on families from Battle Creek, Gull Prairie, and Kalamazoo to help. Perhaps a hundred or more people assembled and worked all day to commands in two languages, for neighboring Potawatomies proved his hardest workers. At day's end the barn stood, and the frolic began.

Early settlers were "farmers by necessity," whatever their skills at home. Timbered land offered the softest soil, and some early settlers sought out heavily wooded bottoms. There, like Caroline Sharpsteen, they might spend a lifetime girdling trees to kill them, then cutting and burning year after year as they slowly carved out cropland. Those who settled on Goguac Prairie or on the oak openings hired teamsters with massive breaking plows and six or seven yoke of oxen to turn the virgin sod and the heavy root systems they called "grubs."

Potatoes kept well and needed no processing, but early settlers preferred corn and wheat, even though they had to husk the corn and thresh the grain and haul it great distances to be ground. Whatever they sowed, they soon learned they must fence the land to preserve their crops from wandering livestock and browsing deer. Wire fencing was unknown. Settlers turned as they had always done to split-rail "zig-zag" fences to surround their crops. With ax, iron wedges, and a wooden beetle to pound them with, a good hand might split 200 rails a day at a penny apiece. One trio made 23,000 rails in 1837. Henry Dwinnell remembered splitting 44,000 for John Bertram and earning enough to pay for 160 acres of government land. Dwinnell went on to become a justice of the peace, and his neighbors called him "Squire."

Each season brought its work. The first crops were harvested by hand—the "armstrong reaper"—as pioneers joked about the back-breaking bending, cutting, binding, and stacking. They threshed wheat with wooden flails on a dirt floor and winnowed it in the wind. They husked corn by hand and kissed the nearest girl for each red ear. The best they saved for next year's seed. Each fall they hunted food or slaughtered what stock they could spare, counting on the cold weather to preserve their meat.

Springtime brought prairie flowers and new neighbors, and the cycle began again. Within a few years each part of the county called itself a neighborhood—its settlers looking to each other for help in good times and comfort in bad. Spontaneous working bees broke the routine of isolated labor and so did festive holidays. By all odds the Fourth of July ranked first among holidays, followed by New Year's Day. Daniel Guernsey fired his pistol out the window on July 4 to please his children in 1833, but by 1835 scores of settlers gathered with Sands McCamly in Battle Creek for speeches, toasts, and feasting. They were joined by several hundred Potawatomies as well. Winter brought good sledding and much visiting about the neighborhood, particularly on New Year's Day. Flutes and fiddles and clapping hands brought out the dancers. Pioneers remembered many such occasions when "Old Granther Morehouse" played "Zip Coon" and "Monnie Musk" on a Jacob Steiner violin already 250 years old.

People gathered for less happy occasions as well. They helped bury the dead and care for the sick when Asiatic cholera swept across the nation in 1832, reaching Detroit in July. It came to Calhoun County soon after, striking Isaac Hurd first in Marshall, where half of 70 residents were stricken and seven died. The town sent its young doctor back to Detroit for medicine and advice, but he himself died on his return, as did missionary Pierce's young wife. Five members of one family died on Dry Prairie before the epidemic passed with cooler weather.

In Clarendon Township in 1833, the settlers offered what comfort they could when Erastus Enos' new stone fireplace collapsed on his sister Polly. In Leroy Township they helped bury Timothy Kelsey's daughter, whose clothing had caught fire as she played near the cooking fire in 1838. James Stanley lived alone with his family in Lee Township in 1835, but when his young son wandered off in the spring of 1837, hundreds of settlers came from miles around to help him search. Days later they found the boy leaning against a tree in a distant swamp, dead. A few months later, Stanley himself died, buried 40 feet deep when his well caved in.

Good times and bad forged isolated settlers'

families into permanent communities. In time these communities began to plan for the future. Almost as soon as the first crops were in, they met in each other's homes for worship and set about building schools for their children. Eliza Ketchum began teaching in Marshall in 1832. Battle Creek settlers floated lumber from Bellevue to finish the school on Goguac Prairie in 1833, where newcomer Warren Shepard marked the trails with colored cloth to help his charges find their way.

Children grew up quickly on the frontier. George Willard read Greek at 14 and taught his first class in Leroy Township at 16. He went to the University of Michigan branch at Kalamazoo and married at 20. He taught in Battle Creek, Marshall, and Coldwater, then became an Episcopal minister in 1848. After teaching at Kalamazoo College during the Civil War, he served in the Michigan Legislature and in Congress. He owned and edited the Battle Creek *Journal* after 1868 and died in 1901.

Anson Van Buren, youngest of nine children, taught himself by firelight until 1838, when he took over the Goguac Prairie school at 17. He, too, studied at the branch university in Kalamazoo and continued teaching in area schools for many years. By the 1870s he was the acknowledged "historian" of Kalamazoo and Calhoun counties, writing often and well for local newspapers and for the state pioneer society.

However strongly they felt about their neighborhoods, the first settlers in western Calhoun County lacked a service center. At first they had to travel for days to Ann Arbor or White Pigeon to find a blacksmith or to grind their grain. They stocked their larders locally with cranberries, blueberries, wild plums, mococks of maple sugar, and game supplied by Potawatomi friends, but had to depend on settled areas of Ohio and Indiana or on Detroit for apples, butter, cheese, and pork. Most of the pioneers had grown up in rural New York or New England where every neighborhood centered around a market town. They expected the same advantages on the frontier.

Emigrants brought few possessions. They knew many pioneering skills, but still looked to mechanics and tradesmen for hardware and glass, lumber, flour, cloth, and dishes. They might make their first furniture with ax and

Everyone found work on pioneer farmsteads as illustrated in this circa 1850 tradesman's cut. Courtesy, Western Michigan University Archives

auger, but they hoped to patronize a local chair turner or wagonmaker as well. Market towns might offer a whole range of necessities and those few luxuries that pioneers missed most.

Town founders tried to locate townsites on key transportation routes in good farming country, for farmers would be their surest customers. They watched for falling streams or river bends where millraces might be dug for waterpower. Calhoun County offered several possibilities, but key locations lay like a string of pearls along the Kalamazoo River. Sydney Ketchum found waterpower sites at Albion and Marshall as early as 1830 and entered them as soon as the land was opened for settlement. Sands McCamly came west in 1831. He saw potential where Battle Creek joined the Kalamazoo and hurried to make his claim at the new land office in White Pigeon. He found J.J. Guernsey ahead of him. Government surveyors Lucius Lyon and Robert Clark had also marked the same land.

Surveyors with an eye for town founding were formidable opponents. Born in Vermont in 1800, Lucius Lyon came to Detroit in 1822. For the next 10 years he would be deputy surveyor general for the district. When the land office opened in White Pigeon in June 1831, he had chosen key locations for himself. He bought the "Big Island" of woods on Prairie Ronde, Michigan's largest prairie in Kalamazoo County. There he platted the village of School- craft. He also interested himself heavily in Kalamazoo and Grand Rapids. He would go on to become Michigan's territorial delegate to Congress in 1833 and then Michigan's first U.S. Senator in 1836. In this case, however, he and Robert Clark accepted McCamly's offer of $100 to step aside.

McCamly formed a partnership with J.J. and Daniel Guernsey to control more than 800 acres at the mouth of Battle Creek. The three men were to meet in Detroit in the fall and invest $6,000 to develop the townsite. Daniel Guernsey had advanced Sherman Comings money to buy land on Toland's Prairie. In return Sherman and his son built Guernsey a cabin that summer at Battle Creek. J.J. Guernsey and his wife visited the site, but his wife refused to live there.

When the partners met again in October, the development plans collapsed. J.J. Guernsey lost interest. Daniel moved to the purchase in 1832, but left the next year. Sands McCamly settled in Marshall, and the power site lay idle; but settlers continued to travel the Territorial Road, which crossed the Kalamazoo at Battle Creek, and to settle the surrounding prairie and oak openings. Samuel Convis bought an interest in the townsite. He came to settle in 1832, as did Moses Hall and Polydore Hudson, the first postmaster. Nathaniel Barney opened a tavern in 1834. His son-in-law, General Ezra Convis, and Sands McCamly then owned the townsite together. Convis agreed to give the water rights to McCamly if he would promise speedy development.

In 1835 McCamly put 20 to 30 men to digging the millrace—"a monument to noble enterprise," E.G. Rust called it—and by November, George Willard said, the area's first clattering up-and-down sawmill "made the frosty woods to echo with its incessant movement." Convis and McCamly printed an elaborate plat map of the village, which circulated widely in the East. Old-timers enjoyed the chagrin of newcomers who compared the ruts and stumps of reality with the plat map's spacious avenues. Nathaniel Barney even told of one asking politely for directions to Battle Creek on the town's main street. Nevertheless, one settler rejoiced, "we have at last a town of our own."

Success or failure of these frontier towns depended partly on location, but chiefly on the determination and capital of the proprietors. Lucius Lyon paid little attention to Schoolcraft; far from waterpower and transportation routes, it lagged for years. Horace Comstock and George Gale went bankrupt developing their own communities in Kalamazoo County. Jesse Crowell in Albion, the Ketchums in Marshall, and Convis and McCamly succeeded. They brought capital, imagination, and staying power.

Ezra Convis had been a militia general in New York and a merchant when hard times sent him west to regain his fortune. Prestige followed him to the new territory. He built the town's first frame house in 1834. He also made his presence felt at Michigan's constitutional convention and served as first house speaker in the legislature. In 1835 he sold his interest in

From his pioneer childhood on, George Willard played a prominent role in Battle Creek's development. He taught a frontier school at 16, served as the minister of St. Thomas Episcopal Church, taught at Kalamazoo College, served in the legislature, and edited the Battle Creek Journal after 1868. Courtesy, Western Michigan University Archives

Battle Creek and turned his attention to the rapids a mile and half upriver. There he founded Verona, for years a successful rival. He died suddenly in 1837, and the legislature named Convis Township for him. Sands McCamly took Convis' place in the legislature and later served as state senator. He continued to live in Battle Creek and did much to develop the town until his death in 1864.

Each of these entrepreneurs recognized that success depended on service to the surrounding settlers. Only Marshall gained security as the county seat, where lawyers, bankers, newspaper editors, and others seeking public business could be expected to make their homes. McCamly, Convis, Crowell, and others like them turned instead to waterpower and transportation improvements, offering manufactured goods and buying raw materials from their neighbors. Similar patterns developed in each of these frontier market towns. Waterpower went first for sawmills, then for grinding grain, and finally for light industry.

Sawmills appeared first in almost every township. Early settlers contented themselves with log cabins, but hoped for board floors and solid roofs over their heads. They needed lumber for building, for furniture, for boxes and barrels, and for a hundred other uses. Sawmills symbolized permanence and progress for early settlers who hauled their fresh-cut lumber across country and dreamed of building "real" frame houses and barns. Local millers threw up

dams or dug races in every conceivable location, sometimes tapping streams so small that wheels turned only a few hours before mill-ponds had to fill again for another day. The 1840 census reported 29 sawmills in the county. These early mills worked slowly as water-wheels drove a "gang" of sawblades up and down through virgin hardwoods, leaving rough vertical saw marks to be planed by hand for finished work. Many an old floorboard and drawer bottom shows traces of these marks today.

Sydney Ketchum built his sawmill at Marshall in 1831. The next year he added a gristmill where dressed millstones broke up corn and wheat into meal, if not fine white "bolted" flour. Sands McCamly built his sawmill in 1835 and also added a gristmill the next season. Ezra Convis followed the same pattern at Verona.

However self-sufficient pioneers might seem, proprietors like McCamly knew they would come to town to repair a plowshare or replace a harness or buy their tea or calico from a local shopkeeper. Each town founder did what he could to bring such services to the community, to improve transportation, particularly by bridging the rivers, and to provide for schools and other public services.

But the success of any town rested also on its citizens. As the people of Galesburg and Comstock discovered, no one person could build a town alone. Fortunately, most early towns-people proved enthusiastic boosters. As Anson Van Buren wrote, "the drones stayed east. None but the working bees came to this new

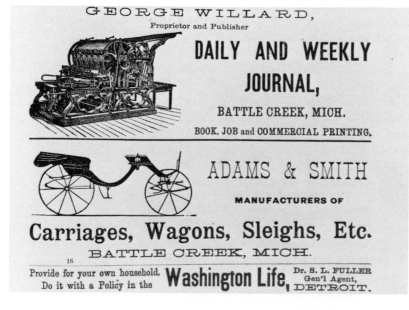

hive of industry in the west."

As the county seat, Marshall fared better than Battle Creek in the early years. Peter Chisholm set up a blacksmith's forge there in 1831. Shoemaker H.C. Goodrich settled in 1832, and Asa Cook made wagons and furniture the same year. H.W. Pendleton arrived in 1833 and began turning chairs and bedsteads on a water-powered lathe. He was joined by another furnituremaker, Lansing Kingsbury. William McCall opened a tailor shop in 1833. Andrew Mann built the National Hotel in 1835—the first brick building in the county, and it still stands today. Lansing Kingsbury built a foundry in 1836, and a fanning-mill factory opened the same year. Marshall recorded 1,200 people on the 1837 census and had brief hopes of being named the state capital.

Like Marshall, Battle Creek continued to offer special services to surrounding farmers. Polydore Hudson opened the town's first store in 1832, hanging his goods from a pole in front of his cabin. David Daniels and William Coleman built a general store in 1835, but Daniels soon left for Verona. The next year Alonzo Noble and Almon Whitcomb started a dry-goods business and began work on a gristmill. These were busy times indeed. Settlers came in tremendous numbers during the great Michigan land boom of the mid-1830s. When that boom ended, 400 people lived in the village itself, and in 1837, according to one historian, Battle Creek boasted "six stores, two taverns, two sawmills, two flouring mills, two machine shops, one cabinet factory and two blacksmith shops."

Calhoun County grew by a third between 1837 and 1840. Many newcomers settled in the villages, and townspeople began to find their own social life. In Battle Creek they met in the log schoolhouse for church services, temperance lectures, or spirited debates on topics of the moment. Middle-class merchants and mechanics built the frame houses and furnishings of longer-settled regions to the east. Boville Shumway opened his store in Marshall in 1835, bringing personal possessions by wagon from the east or buying from local cabinetmakers. He made a bad horse trade, which generated court records giving a picture of some of the comforts of town life. Judge Epaphroditus Ransom heard the case in circuit court in 1839. The dusty case

file still holds a handwritten inventory of Shumway's household goods. He was credited with:

One Secretary, One Piano Forte, One Clock Stowells, One Bureau bedstead, 1 Gilt Looking Glass, 9 Cane-Bottomed fancy chairs, 2 Rocking Chairs, 1 Ingrain Carpet, 2 Cherry Tables, 1 Mahogany dressing table, 1 Wash Stand, 1 China Tea Sett, 12 Cut Tumblers, 1 Castor, 1 Brass Kettle, 2 Lanterns, 5 pair White Blankets, 2 quilts, 1 featherbed, 6 pillow cases, 1 Common Carpet, 4 Common Chairs, 1 pair fire dogs, 1 Dress Table, 4 Pictures.

Clearly, in the villages at least, dirt floors and plank benches were out of fashion. Shumway's pianoforte was valued at $125—about four months' wages for a laborer. His secretary desk was listed at $50 and his bedstead at $75. On the other hand, his "12 Cut Tumblers" were valued at eight cents each and his "fancy chairs" at two dollars apiece.

In 1840 the census-taker recorded another sign of settled country. In the early 1830s newcomers traveled by ox team, joking about their "horned horses," but relying on them for the heavy work of pioneering. When Deacon Solomon Case brought the first team of horses in 1836, Anson Van Buren remembered that Case was "looked up to like a legislator!" Now there were 1,500 lighter, faster, and more stylish horses in the county. The tinkling bells,

Battle Creek village first appeared on this 1838 land-looker's map. Lands to the north remained largely unsettled. The mapmaker optimistically included projected railroad lines, which would not be completed for several years. Courtesy, Western Michigan University Archives

Right: Jeremiah Gardner was the first to enter land in Emmett Township in 1831. He selected choice land in Section 14, near 11-Mile Road. According to the stone set in the gable end, he built this substantial Greek Revival home in 1838. Courtesy, Peter J. Schmitt

Above: Andrew L. Hays was Calhoun County's first doctor and a successful land speculator. He built this Greek Revival mansion of local sandstone in Marshall about 1838, and called it "Locust Hill." Courtesy, Peter J. Schmitt

cans in the War of 1812. Even in the 1830s hundreds camped at the mouth of the creek they called "Waupakisco" on the annual trek to Malden for English annuities. But pioneers remembered many kindnesses. Only two or three times did they hear the dreaded "Kinnapoo Chemokaman," and then only for specific grievances. One settler stole a young brave's greatcoat. He never knew that only by a trader's strenuous pleading did he lose his pig instead of his life in return. Another began digging into a burial mound on his Goguac Prairie farm and was asked to stop so forcefully that he left the country for a year.

Yet, however much settlers appreciated Potawatomi muscle at barn raisings or Potawatomi skill in woodcraft, their ways were different. Whites claimed to own the land "in fee simple" and to do with it what they wished. They called themselves "civilized" and the Potawatomies "savage." They cleared the wilderness and made it farmland. If the Potawatomies wished to camp and hunt, they were trespassers now.

The whites believed absolutely in their government's power to make treaties and to open land for settlement. In the southern part of Calhoun County, they named one township "Tekonsha" after a Potawatomi chief, but it was, after all, their township. In 1836 they platted a village on the St. Joseph River in what their maps said was "section 27" and open to settlement. E.G. Rust recorded in his 1869 history that the village site was "occupied when the whites came to the place, by two or three hundred Indian canvas tents and bark wigwams during the Summer." The Potawatomies

colorful language, and cracking bullwhips were more and more a part of the past and the backcountry.

Eighteen-forty brought a more melancholy ending to the frontier era. Guarded by government troops, local Potawatomies began their long march west of the Mississippi. As one declared, the smoke of Potawatomi wigwams and pioneer cabins would mingle no more in the air over Calhoun County.

Potawatomies knew the best places to hunt and fish and plant their corn. They favored several locations in the county long after the first pioneers began to claim the land under the Treaty of Chicago. All through the 1830s, however, settlers and Potawatomies accommodated each other. There was friction on occasion. Potawatomies fought against the Ameri-

planted eight or ten acres of corn and buried their dead along the river. But the whites dug a millrace through the burying ground, robbing the grave of Chief Tekonquasha.

Governor Lewis Cass felt pressure from all sides to settle "the Indian question." Claiming no animosity himself, he urged the government to remove the Potawatomies as potential British allies should Anglo-American friendship wane. Missionaries like Isaac McCoy and Leonard Slater also urged "removal" to protect their charges from white whiskey, disease, and greed. The government made 17 treaties with Potawatomi groups between 1832 and 1836, offering gifts in exchange for land and urging removal. In the Treaty of Chicago in 1833, the government required Potawatomies to leave Michigan by 1836. Delays followed. Some traveled west under guard. Others fled north to the Ottawas or east to Canada. Most remained where they had always lived, trusting old ways and new friendships with their white neighbors.

In the summer of 1839 Isaac Ketchum called a council at "Notawassippi" in St. Joseph County. He told the gathering, "your Great Father now wants these lands for his white children." In the Western country, he said, "you will be on your own lands and not be trespassers." To drive home his point he declared no further treaty payments would be made "east of the Mississippi."

Muckmote answered for the Potawatomies:

We say again, we will not go. We wish to die where our forefathers died. . . . We are very poor, and one of our nation came back from there and told us that there was no bark to build lodges with, and our women and children would be obliged to live in tents, and it is well known that we are not able to build houses like your white children. Now, there are a great many whites that want us to stay here. They hunt with us and we divide the game, and when we hunt together and get tired we can go to the white men's houses and stay. We wish to stay among the whites, and we wish to be connected with them, and therefore we will not go.

The next winter was hard for everyone. Times were bad again in the summer of 1840, and the Potawatomies were, as trader L. Buell Holcomb wrote, "very uneasy, but said

nothing." Then it happened. Soldiers came and took up nearly all local Potawatomies, following some past the encampment at Duck Lake and on toward Lansing, and cutting off others almost at the Canadian border. They had no easy task, Holcomb reported, for local whites "had quite a feeling over the matter, being in sympathy with the Indians. They would not tell the soldiers where the Indians were if they knew."

Few escaped, and trader Holcomb was hired by the government to accompany the band on the march west. At Skunk's Grove, Illinois, he remembered Moguago, a main chief, crawling away down a gully and eluding the guards. Moguago made his way back to Athens; the others continued the trek. They had to abandon their horses at the Illinois River and make the rest of the trip on smoking steamboats. Far out on the Osage River, the government made its treaty payment—$20 per person for the Calhoun County band. Holcomb wintered in the west and brought 11 Potawatomies back to Athens in the spring of 1841. He later wrote:

All the people were glad to see the Indians. They all said it had been lonesome without them. People thought it was unjust to force them away among the wild western Indians, and onto an open prairie when they had lived all their lives in the woods, and where they could make no maple sugar.

The six surviving families named Holcomb, Norton Hobart, and Thomas Acker their agents to purchase 120 acres of land, livestock, and farm equipment. The little settlement grew to about 40 by 1844, but struggled for many years. Many died of tuberculosis. Others moved for a time to Allegan, then returned. John Moguago died, along with the other original family heads. His nephew, Phineas Pamp-to-pee, served as headman for about 40 residents when N.P. Hobart reported on the settlement in 1878.

Despite the stragglers left at Athens, white settlers could no longer claim they lived in "Indian country." Frontier days were over in Calhoun County. Michigan had become a state, and local people now talked more of distant markets than immediate survival. They waited impatiently for the railroad to reach Marshall and Battle Creek, and they hoped for better times.

CHAPTER II

From Prairie to Prosperity

Battle Creek grew slowly in the early 1840s. The boom days faded, and hard times ruled the land. Dirt streets and scattered buildings changed little from year to year. Most settlers kept busy "making land." They came to town to hunt up a village blacksmith or lay in supplies, and most likely they paid in kind. President Andrew Jackson's "Specie Circular" drained the West of hard cash for land and taxes, and wildcat bank notes bought little or nothing. In these quiet times children grew up learning important skills at home just as their parents had done before them. As far back as anyone could remember, pioneers scattered alone or with their neighbors far ahead of settlement. They worked by hand and sold or traded their surplus to new settlers or local shopkeepers. Town founders chose power sites along the streams with scarcely a thought to transportation routes or distant markets.

But times were changing. Young people in the 1840s would soon discover a world the older generation had never known. The Erie Canal first reduced the time it took to move across the country and cut freighting costs dramatically. A national enthusiasm for "internal improvements" spurred canal projects everywhere. The Michigan Legislature even launched a grand scheme to build a water route from Lake St. Clair to the Kalamazoo River. Yet, however colorful and long remembered in folksong, canalboats belonged to an outmoded technology. Railroads brought the real transportation revolution.

America's first steam locomotive, *Tom Thumb*, chugged into history on the Baltimore & Ohio line in 1830—while Calhoun County pioneers spent weeks traveling from Detroit. Railroads would cut travel time to hours and open distant markets to local businessmen. Frontier leaders saw the benefits immediately. Territorial legislators approved plans for the Pontiac & Detroit Railroad in 1830 and chartered 16 separate ventures, including the Allegan & Marshall, by 1836. Backers of the Erie & Kalamazoo opened 33 miles of track in 1836. Its cars ran from Toledo to Adrian, pulled by a team of horses on four-inch-square wooden rails. The first steam locomotive west of the Alleghenies arrived in January 1837. It pulled a half-dozen cars at 10 miles an hour over the same wooden rails now sheathed with iron straps five-eighths of an inch thick and two-and-a-half inches wide. Passengers expected to get out and walk on the steeper grades. When they rode in open cars, they faced burning cinders and the threat of "snake heads," as trainmen called the strap iron rails that sometimes worked loose and curled up through the cars. Excitement ran high in Adrian; even as far away as Kalamazoo the new line seemed "the great thoroughfare to the West." Legislators hurried plans for three state-sponsored railroads: the Michigan Northern from Port Huron to Grand Rapids, the Michigan Central from Detroit westward, and the Michigan Southern along the old Chicago Military Road.

No matter how devastating the depression of the late 1830s, Battle Creek's residents hoped for better times. Colonel John Berrien had already surveyed the Michigan Central route through the village in 1834. Trains ran along the first 28-mile track from Detroit to Dearborn in 1838. Four engines, five passenger, and ten freight cars hauled nearly 10,000 passengers and two million pounds of freight in the first four months. The rails soon reached Ann Arbor and despite delays ran to Jackson in 1841. One early historian recalled that at Marshall "the first cars were greeted with great enthusiasm" on August 10, 1844.

Emigrants now might leave Detroit at eight in the morning and reach the village, not in weeks or days, but in the afternoon. In 1845 Louisa McOmber traveled west from New York State in 20 days, taking the steamer *Nile* across Lake Erie with 300 passengers, and catching the 8 a.m. train from Detroit. She wrote back to her friends, "I do not like many places on the railroad, for it is laid out of the poorest part of the state generally." She took tea in Marshall and then went on. The countryside looked better as she rode the stagecoach west through Battle Creek. She added, "If you could see some of the great pieces of grain (a great many acres in a piece) and the beautiful farmhouses and orchards, etc., close by, I think you would like the look of them." Sands McCamly wrote a friend that the ticket to Marshall cost $3.50 and the 13-mile stagecoach ride, 62 cents. He added:

We have at the present time in this place the follow-

ing, viz: 17 dry goods and grocery stores, 5 shoe shops, 5 grocery and provision stores, 2 saloons, 2 public houses, 3 churches, 3 flouring mills, 2 woolen factories, 1 furnace, 5 smith shops, 2 saddleries, 1 silversmith, tailoring establishment, pail factory, planing and matching boards, turning wood and iron.

There is a vast amount of business done here besides these already enumerated, saw milling, lathe making, etc., all on a large scale. The place must contain at the present from 1,000 to 1,200 inhabitants. All this has been brought about in, say 8 years. . . .

By this time grading for the rail line had been completed as far as Kalamazoo. Local farmers turned "tie-cutters" all across the county as rail construction brought much-needed cash. On November 25, 1845, the steam locomotive *Battle Creek* pulled the first train into town. As a newspaper editor in Kalamazoo put it, "verily, we are beginning to *live* in this western region; hitherto we have only *stayed* here." The first settlers survived by "beating the bush;" with daily trains, he said confidently, "those, who are coming will catch the bird." Another editor crowed, "who shall anticipate the destiny of this wonderful country?"

But the Michigan Central had its troubles. The first 80 miles of roadbed left much to be desired. Only four depots had been built, and the rails were clearly unsuited to heavy traffic. The state tired of railroad building and, racked with financial problems, sold the line for $2 million in 1846. The state lost $250,000, but private investors agreed to rebuild the road with 60-pound iron "T" rails and to push the tracks west from Kalamazoo.

Construction began again in the spring of 1848. The line reached Niles by October and New Buffalo early the next year. The Michigan Central showed a profit consistently; in 1848 it earned $179,275 on a gross income of $373,981. Passengers paid three to four cents a mile, and freight costs ran about 39 cents per hundred weight over the length of the line.

"The old life is gone and another takes its place" when the railroad comes, said one historian, and villagers looked for dramatic changes. Good times brought new settlers, but many traveled further, following the frontier west or north toward Grand Rapids. Battle Creek grew no faster in the five years after the

Facing page: *Albert Ruger, an itinerant Ohio artist, served in the Civil War, then moved to Battle Creek from 1866 through 1869. He drew this bird's-eye map of the city in 1867, as well as many others for surrounding towns and communities throughout the Midwest. Looking toward the northwest, across the business district, viewers saw their town in the best possible light. Mills along the river and canal show clearly, and the remarkable detail extends even to the distant "octagon" house on North Avenue. Courtesy, Michigan Room, Willard Public Library*

trains than in the five years before. Towns along the railroad did gain importance as railheads for their neighbors. Heavy freight arrived for transfer to other parts of the county. Local farmers brought their bulky crops to warehouses for shipment east.

Most Calhoun County settlers, like most Americans, were farmers in the 1840s. Village blacksmiths repaired their plows. Local sawmills turned their logs into lumber, and the county's 29 mills ranked fourth in number in the state in 1840. Water-powered gristmills ground grain for feed and unbolted flour for local needs. The county ranked third in the number of such mills in 1840 and produced more than 16,000 barrels of flour. John Palmer and Charles Gray built a tannery just months after the first trains steamed into the village. They bought their first hide for $1.50 and sold the leather for $6 as belts to drive local machinery. But local entrepreneurs were no longer limited by local needs. With the railroad they could use their skills to develop new products marketable nationwide. The next years were busy in Battle Creek.

Erastus Clark was 45 and a "joiner," as they called skilled woodworkers, but he wrote in a bold, clear hand. In 1850 he was named assistant marshal to record the federal census in Battle Creek. In the last days of July, he walked each dusty street asking people their names and ages, occupations and birthplaces. On August 2 he reached the 198th dwelling—the hotel where he himself boarded. On great folio sheets he had written the names of 1,050 people, ranging from month-old James Gorham, the cooper's son, to Martha Anderson, the village elder at 77. Battle Creek had doubled in size during the decade, but still trailed Marshall, the county seat. Most people walked wherever they went in this country village. Only one family in five kept a horse. On the other hand, more than half owned a milk cow, and 35 people living inside the village still listed themselves as "farmers."

Yet the little village already reflected the complex division of labor that marked modern industrialization. Clark recorded 312 men in 57 different occupations. Nineteen admitted they were "laborers." Others followed a wide range of trades from "goldsmith" and "gunsmith" to "tinner" and "teacher." As might be expected

in a service community, 16 merchants and 17 clerks kept shop. Another 17 were blacksmiths. Nine were lawyers and six physicians. The building boom in Battle Creek kept 27 carpenters and 10 masons busy.

Four men called themselves "manufacturers." Many more indicated they were patternmakers, machinists, joiners, furnacemen, moulders, and other factory workers. Erastus Clark carried several census schedules with him. He used a "Products of Industry" sheet whenever he found someone making more than $500 worth of goods per year. Nineteen firms produced goods valued at $142,000 in all. Most employed two or three workers and paid them $25 to $30 a month. In these early days, four companies used waterpower, but 15 relied on human strength alone. None invested in costly steam engines or horsepower. Most used local raw materials and made goods attractive to local customers. For example, Samuel Adams assembled 14 guns worth an average of $20 each and repaired others. Silas Dodge fashioned 1,400 axes at $1.50 each, as well as drawknives and augers at his Edge Tool works. Four carriagemakers made 62 buggies, wagons, and sleighs. One firm, Adams & Smith, accounted for more than half that total. Marcus Adams had come to Battle Creek in 1844 and paid $75 for half-interest in a wagon works begun eight years earlier. Smith joined him in 1849, and the newly styled firm launched a long and prosperous career. Moved from Marshall in 1848, the Nichols & Shepard foundry was the town's largest employer, keeping a dozen men busy at general jobbing and casting 500 plows. In addition, the firm made six steam engines and $2,000 worth of metal gearing.

Not everyone produced for local consumption alone. During the census year, the town's three shoemaking establishments turned local leather into 7,592 pairs of boots and shoes. William Wallace and Charles Mason each ran woolen mills weaving local fleece into nearly 60,000 yards of cloth. Mason had arrived with his family in 1841 and bought an interest in what may have been the state's first woolen mill, begun by James Marduss in 1839. William Wallace had come two years later after a successful career as a mill operator in Vermont. According to a newspaper account in 1855, both firms were working at capacity. Wallace then had 20 hands and produced 5,000 yards of cloth. He also bought a quarter of a million pounds of fleece for shipment east. Mason ran two machines with 320 spindles. His 22 employees carded 18,000 pounds of wool and wove 30,000 yards of cassimere, tweed, flannel, and jean, which he sold as far away as St. Louis, Chicago, and Detroit at an average of 75 cents a yard.

Clark found that the five largest firms produced two-thirds of the goods. Nichols & Shepard and the two woolen mills accounted for one-third and the town's two flour mills the other. At his three-year-old White Mill on the Battle Creek, N.J. Cushman turned out 6,500 barrels of flour valued at four dollars each. Jonathan Hart's new mill added another 6,000 barrels. Ideally situated in the heart of Michigan's wheat belt, Battle Creek would flourish as a flour-milling center for many decades.

Two of Battle Creek's most successful businessmen operated lard oil mills in 1850. Richard Titus had been a sea captain in the South American trade before coming to the village with a group of Quaker settlers in 1843. He joined with Jonathan Hart to found one of the state's first lard oil refineries. In the days before kerosene, Americans pushed away the darkness with open oil lamps or tallow candles. Fat pork could be pressed to yield an inexpensive substitute for whale oil, and both men saw sufficient market to continue separately when they dissolved their partnership in 1847. In 1850 Hart pressed 3,000 gallons of oil; Titus produced another 130 barrels. Both firms together made 33,500 pounds of candles.

Midway through his count of village households, Clark came to Lois Androus, struggling to make ends meet with her four children. For extra income, Androus took in three young boarders, all of whom would figure prominently in Battle Creek's history. Moses Sutton, 26, ran a daguerreotype studio; Myron H. Joy had just begun his law practice. The third boarder grew up near Goguac Prairie and traveled about the region; returning in 1849, Anson Van Buren took charge of the Battle Creek High School with his landlady's daughter for the first student. His predecessor, Presbury Moore, caught the gold fever and left for California.

Van Buren arranged with Erastus Hussey to hold his school in the Union Block. He taught all students with one assistant, telling them that everyone had something to say. "You must teach your pen to talk," he said, "that is all there is of writing." Van Buren used his "talking pen" to give us indelible glimpses of early Battle Creek. The village as he saw it then was less than 20 years old, yet boasted seven dry-goods shops and a drugstore clerked by William Andrus. William Brooks ran the hardware store and served as village president. Alfred Starkweather was the grocer. Walter Woolnough came in 1845 to open a newspaper office. A dentist, a tailor, and a jeweler also kept shop downtown.

We cannot know for certain what Van Buren and his neighbors saw on their storekeepers' shelves. But we do know what Mumford Eldred's customers found when they came to his general store west of town. Eldred went

Rev. George Willard served this little church for several years. He went on to become an influential newspaper editor. Courtesy, Larry B. Massie

FREE LECTURE!

SOJOURNER TRUTH,

Who has been a slave in the State of New York, and who has been a Lecturer for the last twenty-three years, whose characteristics have been so vividly portrayed by Mrs. Harriet Beecher Stowe, as the African Sybil, will deliver a lecture upon the present issues of the day,

At   On

And will give her experience as a Slave mother and religious woman. She comes highly recommended as a public speaker, having the approval of many thousands who have heard her earnest appeals, among whom are Wendell Phillips, Wm. Lloyd Garrison, and other distinguished men of the nation.

☞ At the close of her discourse she will offer for sale her photograph and a few of her choice songs.

bankrupt in 1852, and the court required a complete inventory of his stock. In faded script on 26 folio pages, the appraisers made a shopping list of 832 different items, giving quantities and values totaling nearly $3,000. Eldred lined his shelves with every need from hardware to tea and spices, from schoolbooks to boots and shoes. There were needles and thread, thimbles and half a hundred pieces of cloth, but also ready-made silk and linen handkerchiefs, seven kinds of cravats, silk mittens, and china fans. There were caps and hats, fishhooks and pocketknives for young shoppers, as well as ivory whistles, rubber balls, and even a dozen India rubber doll's heads.

Twenty-one different women's hat styles and 16 hats and caps for men waited in one corner, alongside parasols, India shawls, veils, and vests. The appraisers noted carpentry tools of all kinds, log chains, nails, screws, paints, and window glass, beside family bibles, pens, perfumes, and toothbrushes. Coffee cost a dime a pound and opium a dollar an ounce. Glass dishes and tumblers came cheap as did familiar "blue-edged" plates, but a 44-piece "Mullbury tea set" cost $3.44. From bedcords and bush scythes, hatpins and horse shears, to quinine and carpetbags, the appraisers listed everything, even 78 suspenders and one lot of shawls behind the safe. From their catalog we can see the vast array of merchandise available to shoppers in the 1850s.

"The railroad and the telegraph had given a wonderful impetus to the town," said Van Buren, adding that "the railroad had so far annihilated distance that we were now in the suburbs of Detroit and Chicago." Traveling entertainers and lecturers came by train, but Van Buren remembered that villagers made most of their own entertainment. As Benjamin Franklin and his friends had done in Philadelphia a century earlier, local tradesmen made "visiting" a high art. Van Buren paid men like Dr. John Balcomb, Erastus Hussey, George Willard, and Chandler Ford the highest tribute when he called them "learned." They opened lively discussions with "what have you read since we last met?" and pooled the village's store of knowledge.

Van Buren particularly valued his contacts with strong-willed, even eccentric people who made lasting impressions. Most had little recognition outside their own neighborhoods, but in 1856 one such figure came to Battle Creek who would be known nationwide even today. Six-foot, turbaned, pipe-smoking, this black woman gathered her family around her in Battle Creek or nearby Harmonia, selling blackberries, cooking, cleaning, taking in washing, caring for the sick—and lecturing.

Harriet Beecher Stowe once said, "an audience was what she wanted—it mattered not whether high or low, learned or ignorant. She had things to say, and was ready to say them at all times and to anyone." Coming out of 18th-century New York, of indeterminate age, her Battle Creek friends called her a child of the Revolution. She grew up a slave and saw her children separated from her. When she was freed she took a new name—"Sojourner Truth," because she "was to travel up and down the land, showin' the people their sins— an' bein' a sign unto them." In the course of her long life she traveled throughout the East and Midwest speaking out against injustice and in favor of reforms of many kinds. Her quietest words could still a crowd, and those who opposed her ideas trembled when she came. "I will speak upon the ashes," she said when Indi-

ana opponents planned to burn one meeting-house. In a more famous instance, she spoke so powerfully in 1858 that a doctor in the audience challenged her to prove she was not a man in woman's clothing. Speaking of the white children she had nursed in slavery, she unbuttoned her dress, telling the crowd it was to their shame, not hers.

While others preached to the sheep, she found herself speaking often to the goats, as she did one night for hours to quiet a mob that threatened a revival meeting. She spoke more firmly as the years advanced. In 1863 she told Harriet Beecher Stowe, "The Lord has made me a sign unto this nation, an' I go round a-testifyin.'" She visited Abraham Lincoln the next year to argue the needs of freedmen. Later

Local artist Frank C. Courter completed this portrait of Sojourner Truth and Abraham Lincoln in 1893. Commissioned by Sojourner's close friend Francis Titus, the large oil painting was first exhibited at the Columbian Exposition in Chicago, where it hung in the Michigan Building. Mrs. Titus presented the imposing canvas to the Battle Creek Sanitarium, where it was destroyed by fire in 1902. Courtesy, Michigan Room, Willard Public Library

she championed the rights of women and was named one of three Michigan delegates to the first Woman's Rights Convention in Rochester, New York. Whether in Battle Creek or on the road, she worked to support herself and her family. When she sold pictures of herself in the 1860s, she called it selling "the shadow to support the substance." She also sold her biography, later revised by her longtime friend Frances Titus. She once told Horace Greeley, "I am a self-made woman," but she never forgot her friends around the country. In 1870 she made a farewell tour through the East, telling her audiences, "I may never come this way again." The next year she was off to lecture in Kansas, and she continued to speak out for many years.

Michigan allowed women to vote in 1872, if they could read. Refused by the clerk in Battle Creek, Sojourner Truth answered acidly, "I tell you, I can't read a book, but I can read the people." The people responded when she died in 1883. Messages and gifts came from every-

Fire engines and horses were once kept on the first floor of the old city hall. Battle Creek residents were proud of their gleaming "steam pumper." Courtesy, Michigan Room, Willard Public Library

where. Prominent merchants like Edwin Nichols and T.B. Skinner were pallbearers, and a thousand people viewed the casket where she lay in black with her classic Quaker cap. Her friends buried her on the high ground in Oak Hill Cemetery. Later they raised a six-foot column in her memory not 40 feet from C.W. Post's lofty mausoleum. Sojourner Truth's marker says she was 105. Other people thought she was older or younger, perhaps only a little over 80. Her age was immaterial—she counted her years from emancipation in 1828—her ideas and her call to speak them mattered more. Perhaps most people understood her best when she responded to a critic just before the Civil War. He said he never minded her talk anymore than a flea bite. "Perhaps not," she answered, "but the Lord willing, I'll keep you scratching!"

Sojourner Truth moved to Battle Creek in boom times. The town would more than triple in size in the 1850s. By the end of the decade its citizens demanded wider recognition. Myron Joy, editor Walter Woolnough, Leonidas Dibble, and Joseph Babcock drafted a charter and called on the legislature to make them a city. Dibble, Erastus Hussey, and others tried unsuccessfully to rename the town "Waupakisco" as the Potawatomies called the creek. Modern historian Berenice Lowe pictured a village charter encumbered by such trivial regulations as those prohibiting nude bathing, hoop rolling, and kite flying downtown. The new city charter, on the other hand, proved an austere 40-page document that provided for the regular succession of government and addressed 19th-century concerns for the common peace, safety, and morality.

Fire in public places frightened city dwellers more than anything else. The common council was to provide for fire-fighting companies and to require householders to keep fire equipment ready. Council members were also expected to require that all downtown buildings be built of brick. They were to regulate construction of chimneys, party walls, "and other things that may be dangerous." In particular, the city was to oversee "construction of all blacksmith shops, cooper shops, carpenter shops, planing establishments, bakeries, and all buildings and establishments usually regarded as extra hazardous in respect to fire."

With the town growing so rapidly, people also worried about public health. The council should keep livestock and dogs from running loose, regulate burying the dead, and provide for clearing debris from local watercourses. In particular, the council was to prevent people from dumping "filthy and other matter" into the water for the sake of health and decency. Citizens must keep their sidewalks clear of "snow, ice, dirt, mud, boxes, and every encumbrance or obstruction thereon." The city marshal was "to compel the owner or occupant of any grocery, soap, or candle factory, butcher's shop, stall, stable, barn, privy, sewer, or other unwholesome or nauseous house or place, to cleanse or remove the same."

Townspeople wanted assurances that public decency would prevail. They expected the council to punish "all lewd and lascivious behavior in the streets." They wanted regulation of saloons, billiard halls, and bowling alleys, and suppression of riots. In particular, they wanted to suppress "disorderly houses, houses of ill-fame, and houses of assignation." They wanted gunfire and gaming forbidden and the Sabbath kept. The council was to provide for honest services by establishing a farmer's market with licensed stalls, by measuring all firewood offered for sale, and by regulating parking and "immoderate riding or driving." The charter took effect in February 1859. In April voters elected cattle buyer E.W. Pendill, the first of many businessmen to serve as mayor, and named other merchants like Erastus Hussey as aldermen.

One measure of a town's prosperity is its building activity. Where 37 carpenters and masons worked in 1850, 137 built the houses of 1860. Dr. W.G. Saunders found not 200 dwelling houses but 760 on the city streets, among them that of 53-year-old broommaker John Kellogg, his wife Ann, and their seven children, the youngest of whom, Will K. Kellogg, was barely a month old. Saunders also found James White, 38, and his wife Ellen, 31. He listed White as a "Second Advent Clergyman" but could hardly anticipate the later importance of these two families. He counted 3,508 people for the census in 1860. He asked the "profession, occupation or trade of each person, male or female, over 15 years of age." The specialization evident in 1850 continued as 1,230 workers listed 128 different kinds of work. Some continued at the earlier trades. The number of merchants grew from 16 to 26 and the number of clerks from 17 to 69 as stores increased their trade. Some of the old service jobs like blacksmithing and tailoring lost ground in the shift to industry. There were well-diggers and stump-pullers in town now, and marble-cutters, nurserymen, and artists, bakers and brewers and broommakers, even a "healing medium" and a half-dozen music teachers.

Women made up 18 percent of the work force. Two hundred twenty-one women told the census taker they worked out, but most held jobs in two or three traditional fields. More than half said they did "housework." The others taught school or worked in the clothing industry as dressmakers, milliners, or weavers. Every clerk in town was male, and most other paid jobs went to men. The census taker liked to use the suffix "ess" to designate women working in jobs usually held by men, calling a man a "tailor" and several women "tailoresses." He listed 14 male "physicians" and called 40-year-old Martha Parble a "doctoress." Two women did work as "printers," and Mary Havens "loaned money." Another was an artist along with her husband, and Saunders listed English-born Mary Smith as "fortune teller."

Men controlled wealth as well as work. Most put their assets in hundreds rather than thousands of dollars, but 40-year-old Loyal Kellogg told Saunders he had $100,000 in real estate and $50,000 in personal property. Land broker Sands McCamly trailed far behind with $35,000, as did money-lender Merritt Coleman and wool merchant William Wallace with $30,000. Saunders found 734 families in Battle Creek. A few weeks earlier the tax assessor enrolled 661 people for real estate and another 51 for personal property. Again Loyal Kellogg paid the highest tax at $206. Several men owed $50 to $100 in 1860 and some even more. Mrs. Aurelia Havens, widow of the town druggist and wealthiest woman taxpayer, had been assessed $86.80 on $6,200 in personal property.

Heated political discussion and talk of secession marked the fall of 1860. Winter brought its round of chores on nearby farms as people looked toward spring planting. Diary entries in April spoke of cabbages and corn and "choar-

Right: *The Harrison Granite Company of Barre, Vermont was chosen to complete this statue honoring Civil War and Spanish-American War veterans in 1899. The statue itself was called "Defense of the Flag." It was cast in one-inch-thick bronze, stood seven feet high, and weighed two tons. With its granite base, it reached 35 feet high when it was installed in Monument Square at Michigan and Division in 1901. Fifteen thousand people came to the dedication and Memorial Day parade—the largest such gathering in the city's history. Courtesy, Peter J. Schmitt*

Below: *This photo of Battle Creek just after the Civil War shows wide streets little used by horses and wagons. Greek Revival homes and wooden fences date from the city's pioneer period. Courtesy, Michigan Room, Willard Public Library*

ing about" even while the guns boomed at Fort Sumter. Preoccupied with seasonal tasks, most diarists made no comment on Lincoln's April 15 call for volunteers. Stephen Earl went to church on the 21st to hear the elder preach "that Washington was in the hands of the Southern Army," but noted only "it has been a fine day and the most like Spring of any we have had yet." Others mentioned nothing until the 30th, when they went to town to see the first volunteers away.

Townspeople caught the enthusiasm more quickly. Marshall Mayor Charles Dibble had business in New York. His wife told him in a newsy letter on April 19, "the music of the fife and the drum is almost constantly heard in the streets." Seventy men had volunteered, she said, adding, "the war excitement has quite displaced the smallpox." Not everyone favored Lincoln's call for troops; she found one man "perfectly rampant on war matters, on the secession side of course." In Battle Creek Walter Woolnough had no doubts. The staunch Republican editor told his *Journal* readers, "a man is either a Patriot or a traitor—if the latter, he had better keep it to himself."

Confusion reigned despite enthusiasm in Battle Creek. Telegrams flew back and forth to Lansing. Leonidas Dibble raised 75 volunteers in the first 10 days, but wrote on April 19, "we are entirely in the dark as to what course to pursue, awaiting directions from Headquarters." The Marshall Light Guards joined the First Michigan Volunteer Infantry and marched off to leave their dead on the field at Bull Run. The Battle Creek Artillery left under Captain Cornelius Byington with the Second Michigan Infantry. Many young men expected the Rebellion to end by harvest time, though Michigan's Governor Austin Blair reminded them in May that many who left "joyously singing the national anthem" would come home in a "bloody shroud." Ultimately Calhoun County sent 3,878 men to war, including 53 black men.

The war came home to Battle Creek as letters filtered back. Convalescent soldiers came home as well, visible reminders of disease and distant battles. Repeated calls for more men brought a steady stream of enlistments, while women and children ran the farms or kept their homes in town. As weeks passed into months, tedious waiting and wasting disease dampened enthusiasm. When young men responded, local citizens encouraged them with $100 of city money as a bounty. They also paid extra county taxes to support needy families.

Most responded as individuals to what they saw around them. Bedford farmers brought 63 loads of firewood for soldiers' families in January 1864, when a load represented a week's pay. Loyal Kellogg agreed to donate 25 pounds of flour for every load, and the Bedford farmers promptly returned with 37 more. Such generosity helped in a time of rising prices, as corn, beef, and firewood doubled. Flour prices swung widely, reaching $7 a barrel in 1863,

Above: *One of the earliest photographs of downtown Battle Creek shows Jefferson Avenue in 1868. Cows milling in the distance would soon be kept off the streets by city ordinance Courtesy, Michigan Room, Willard Public Library*

Left: *Wool and wheat were major crops on thrifty area farms in the 1860s and 1870s. Courtesy, Western Michigan University Archives*

and $12 the next year, falling in 1865, then rising to $15 in 1867.

The papers carried war news and announcements of sanitary fairs, but Gerald Herdman concluded that life went on much as it always had. The town supported a variety of activities during the war. People turned out for county agricultural fairs and the three-day exhibitions of the Agricultural and Mechanical Association in 1861 and 1863. Ralph Waldo Emerson lectured in 1854, 1860, 1863, and 1866. He thought most Michigan settlers "rough, grisly Esaus, full of dirty strength," but he found in

Battle Creek a group of "loving New Englanders who cherish the lyceum." The *Journal* regularly announced traveling lecturers, musicians, and dramatic troupes as well as local talent. Eight different circuses set up their tents, advertising polar bears, elephants, and buffalo, along with performing dogs and monkeys.

More children went to school, for despite enlistments, the county grew steadily. Private tutors taught music and other arts, but the number of regular schoolteachers in the county increased from 295 in 1860 to 391 in 1865. Gerald Herdman notes that women held half the positions in 1860 and 85 percent in 1864. They earned far less than men because, said one school inspector, local officials had not yet "learned the dishonesty of withholding an equal compensation from female teachers for equal services rendered."

Congress inaugurated a number of special fees and taxes to help reduce government debt in 1862. Deputy Internal Revenue Service assessors in each congressional district compiled monthly lists of men and women affected. Some, like doctors and lawyers, bought licenses. Piano and melodeon owners faced an instrument tax of two to six dollars a year, and carriage owners paid a special fee. Farmers and butchers paid to slaughter livestock, while photographers pasted tax stamps on the backs of their pictures.

Four out of five people in Battle Creek made less than $600 a year, but those who earned more were taxed on their "surplus income." Local newspapers published names and incomes to encourage honesty. Vigilant assessors recorded substantial penalties and sometimes took reluctant reporters to court. One hundred thirty-nine people reported taxable income in 1862. Of these, 19 earned more than $1,000, yet these 19 accounted for 42 percent of the $78,836 recorded, averaging $1,767 each. The others trailed far behind with an average of $377. Battle Creek prospered over the next years, and "surplus income" for investments grew. In 1863 William Wallace owned the woolen mill. He and wholesale merchant Thomas Skinner gained 18 percent of all income between them. Forty-seven percent went to the 13 who reported over $1,000. One hundred twenty others again averaged $378. The number of taxpayers rose to 186 by 1864. With more entering the list for the first time, 150 paid tax on $1,000 or less, averaging $362. Thirty-six people averaged $2,000 and accounted for 57 percent of everything reported. The pattern continued in 1865: 157 averaged only $319, while the top 29 earned 55 percent of the total and averaged $2,140 each.

By the end of the Civil War, the old "pioneer democracy" had faded, and Battle Creek's residents could be divided into low, middle, and upper income groups. Interestingly enough, the income tax lists bear little relation to social standing. No teachers, few lawyers, and only

an occasional physician reported any taxable income at all. The records do show which manufacturers kept the highest profit margin and how much capital had been concentrated in the hands of 15-20 percent of the population. By 1865 four men reported $4,000 or more. Three were bankers and one a merchant. Banker and miller Loyal Kellogg indicated $3,800. Foundrymen John Nichols, his son Edwin, and Thomas Shepard each claimed $2,000. Successful bankers, merchants, or manufacturers had money to invest in peacetime expansion.

Business activities also came to life in the same faded tax lists. In May 1863, when the war was at its height, 32 firms paid *ad valorem* taxes on goods produced each month. Five made flour barrels; another half-dozen made wagons. Three harnessmakers turned Oakley & Badgley leather into useful articles, as did four shoe factories. James Upton, David Coy, and the Nichols & Shepard foundry built farming equipment, particularly threshing machines. One candlemaker, a sash and door company, two furniture makers, and a wood pump manufacturer reported as did John Kellogg, broommaker.

By war's end the monthly lists numbered 48 establishments—a 50-percent increase. Many of these new companies offered everyday goods and services, but some provided hints of luxury. Three photographers paid their tax, as did a trunk maker and a tombstone cutter. The clothing industry boomed. At a time when wages averaged a dollar or two a day, the town's four clothing factories each did $600-$800 business every month. Good rail connections and access to hardwood brought one new company all the way from New Hampshire: Willard Jefts made patented "extension tables" in 1864 and slowly built his business to an important postwar industry.

Farm life and farm products still gave direction to Battle Creek's most active firms. Richard Titus and Jonathan Hicks ran the familiar Peoples' Mill, and Loyal Kellogg owned both the Red Mill and the White Mill. With two smaller competitors, they accounted for 56,000 of the county's 183,046 barrels of flour in 1863. The county led the state in flour production throughout the decade.

Oakley & Badgley's tannery and the Wallace

Woolen Mill ranked among the town's most active industries. William Wallace consistently led the rest, with $2,000-$5,000 in business every month. Implement makers produced hay rakes, grain cradles, and threshing machines. Nichols & Shepard, makers of the Vibrator thresher, ranked second to Wallace on the monthly lists, followed by James Upton and Dorr Burnham, who also made locally patented sawmill machinery.

The monthly records show business booming for these successful firms through 1864 and 1865. After the war Wallace, Nichols & Shepard, Burnham, and Upton continued to prosper with monthly business rising well into 1866. Loyal Kellogg owned a cooper shop turning out the barrels he needed for his flour mills. His cooper shop alone averaged more than $1,400 worth of barrels a month to place him

fourth among manufacturers.

Battle Creek businessmen entered the postwar years on a wave of optimism. While inflation continued, new opportunities beckoned, and some dreamed of greatness. Yet the next 20 years saw many overextend themselves and crash, while others mastered the new techniques of corporate structure, finance, and product innovation that marked the coming of really big industry to the town.

Loyal Kellogg may have been the town's first millionaire. With his banking interests, his flour mills, and his cooper shop, he stood ready to capitalize on peacetime markets. Yet the records show his cooper shop suddenly failing

in the summer of 1866. Later he lost his mills to Marshall banker Horace Perrin and lived as a bitter recluse for nearly 40 years. Kellogg had opened a private bank in 1851 and soon acquired his two mills and cooper shop. A flamboyant and popular figure, Kellogg loved fine horses and lived well, but he also led his own coopers in the town's first strike. Together they marched from shop to shop until all barrelmakers agreed to higher wages. He helped organize the First National Bank and was named its first president in June 1865. Berenice Lowe suggests he tried to corner the New York wheat market the very next winter. For months he held 44,000 barrels of flour in

Above: *A New York phrenologist, Orson Fowler, popularized the octagon style of building in* A Home for All, *which he published in 1849. In the next 20 years, many people around the country turned to this daring new style. Ten of these octagons still stand in Calhoun County, including this one at 159 North Avenue. Courtesy, Peter J. Schmitt*

Left: *Several area farmers built octagon houses in the prosperous 1850s and 1860s. Octagon-shaped buildings represented the most radical architectural thinking of the time. Three octagons once stood in Battle Creek; only one survives. Courtesy, Western Michigan University Archives*

Right: *In 1869, the new brick Potter House proclaimed prosperous times in Battle Creek. Its renaissance styling suited the mood of midcentury businessmen. Courtesy, Western Michigan University Archives*

Above: *A.C. Hamblin's lavish opera house held 1,200 people when it was completed in 1868. The slate-roofed Second Empire building brought a new and urban atmosphere to Main Street. The mansard-roofed city hall stands nearby. Courtesy, W.K. Kellogg Foundation*

cheese and butter making. He kept a milk herd of 85 cattle and bought from his neighbors, making butter from the cream with a 10-horsepower steam engine to power his churns. He made his cheese from the skimmed milk. R.C. Kedzie of the Agricultural College analyzed samples and reported, "I was much surprised to find that so good and *toothsome* a cheese could be made from skim-milk." In his first season White produced 17,318 pounds of butter and 47,237 pounds of cheese. The state board of agriculture published a special tribute to his success. As time went on he added a spur track from the Michigan Central line half a mile away and arranged to have "White's Station" an official stop. Four out of five Calhoun County farmers owned less than 100 acres in 1870, but the census taker credited White with 880 and valued his property second highest in the county at $132,000. He kept 18 horses, 80 dairy cows, another 80 steers and heifers, and 100 pigs fed on factory wastes. He had fenced his land into great fields of wheat, corn, oats, and barley, and he stood almost alone in the county as a pioneer "agribusinessman." White lived much of the time in Marshall and left the management of his operation to others. As he found it hard to keep up the quality, his pioneer cheese factory fell on hard times. By the early 1870s he was embroiled in a dozen lawsuits, and he failed to survive the financial panic of 1873.

Not everyone overreached themselves in the booming postwar years. Signs of solid prosperity soon appeared on Battle Creek streets. Builders worked hard to close in the Andrus Block in 1867. With the new building, William Andrus repaid the town for its confidence years before. He had come as a child with his parents in 1835 and gone to work in Allan Havens' drugstore for 10 years. When Havens died in 1852, Andrus bought the store for $4,300 with the good will of local businessmen and $72 of his own money. Now the Andrus Block would house the Masonic Temple and the finest drugstore outside Detroit.

Mayor Erastus Hussey and the city council approved a $12,000 bond issue for the new city hall in 1867. Incoming mayor William Wallace watched over construction the next year. The new city hall would be three stories high and built of brick, an imposing mansard-roofed

Detroit and Chicago while prices rose to $20 a barrel in New York. But he waited too long. When he finally delivered in the spring, the prices had fallen to $12. He lost well over $300,000 and, says Lowe, he never recovered. Over the next few years his creditors demanded satisfaction, and the sheriff began auctioning Kellogg property. Marshall banker Horace Perrin sued Kellogg, William Wallace, and several other defendants in 1870. The case dragged on until Kellogg lost an appeal to Michigan's supreme court in 1879.

Other entrepreneurs tried new products. When wool prices dropped after the war, many area farmers slaughtered their flocks. Some turned to dairying. In nearby Emmett Township, gentleman farmer Charles White invested $20,000 to build the state's largest and most modern cheese factory. He dammed the Kalamazoo River, dug a millrace, and built a two-story wooden factory 32 by 100 feet. New Yorker Leander Durkee came to manage his

building in the Second Empire style so popular in cities around the country. It would bring together all city functions under a single roof. People might climb three flights of stairs to public meetings on the top floor. The second housed offices and space where the council or the court could hold sessions while the smell of fire horses drifted up from down below. The city jail stood just behind.

In July 1868 the papers reported, "men and women have been at their wits' end to keep cool," and added, "cool linen, cool shades, and cool drinks all afford but partial relief" when temperatures reached 106 degrees. Water in the millrace fell; local millers used the time to make repairs and waited for better weather. In spite of the heat, the papers reported "two fine business blocks, that of Nelson Eldred, corner of Main and Jefferson, and that of A.C. Hamblin on Main Street West—are rapidly going up." Hamblin spent $40,000 on his lavish mansard opera house. He combined two large storefronts and a 1,200-seat auditorium, the largest in the region.

The next year Henry Potter built a four-story, red-brick hotel near the depot and modestly claimed "a *cuisine* unsurpassed by any house on the railroad between Kalamazoo and Jackson." Leonidas Dibble headed a new railroad company that laid its first track in 1869. The 232-mile Chicago & Lake Huron line was finished by 1873 at a cost of more than $12 million. It linked Battle Creek with Lansing and with Valparaiso, Indiana, offering competitive freight rates with the Michigan Central.

Fifty-eight hundred thirty-eight people lived in Battle Creek by 1870—1,234 families with 1,732 school-age children. The town owned three "ward schools" but began a new $90,000 central school building in May 1870. The new school seated 864 children in 18 classrooms and included a music room, a library, and a museum. The ventilating system exchanged fresh heated air several times an hour in every room.

The census taker reported that Battle Creek doubled Marshall's growth. The county seat fell behind and would never again equal its western rival. Marshall held fifth place among Michigan cities in 1850; in 1870 it ranked 16th. Industry made the difference. Battle Creek now claimed a third of all manufacturing establish-

ments in the county and well over half the factory workers. Eighty-two companies employed 716 workers in Battle Creek, while Marshall claimed a third of that number in 56 firms. Battle Creek tripled Marshall's annual output and capital investment.

Local businesses faltered after the "Black Friday" panic on Wall Street in 1869. Hard times continued through the early 1870s. Nevertheless, solidly established companies carried on and provided the industrial base for future growth. No firm demonstrates that staying power better than the Nichols & Shepard foundry. Old-timers remembered John Nichols as a strong man who worked beside his men in the first small shop on Canal Street—doing general blacksmithing and making plowshares for the local market. Nichols went to the California goldfields for a time and sent his young son Edwin to "rough it" in Nebraska for his health. Both returned by the mid-1850s to give their lifetimes to the business.

The company made its first steam engine in 1854 and turned out 11 the next year at $2,000 each. Edwin Nichols joined David Shepard and his father as general manager in 1859. Under his direction 16 men made plows and other farm machinery, including the first 11 "Vibrator" threshing machines. Crowds gathered in 1861 to watch one Vibrator machine leave for Stockton, California, where it won a premium for its contribution to mechanized farming. The company patented the Vibrator in 1862, and business boomed. Incorporated in 1867, Nichols, Shepard & Company moved two years later to sprawling new quarters on the rail lines east of downtown. By 1874 one hundred fifty men made five threshers a day in season. Three years later the company marketed its machines

High school classes met on the third floor of the central school building. Courtesy, Western Michigan University Archives

in every state in the country. A 110-horsepower steam engine now powered woodworking machines as well as heavy metal shears and automatic punches. Three hundred men used two million feet of lumber in 1,500 threshers, horsepower machines, and other farm equipment.

In 1880 Nichols & Shepard produced 947 Vibrators, 488 horsepower machines, and 216 portable engines worth $787,000. Skilled workers earned $2.25 for a 10-hour day and laborers $1.50. The company took a paternal interest in its employees, selling nearby lots and houses to married workers at reasonable terms, providing longtime employees with company stock, and organizing a variety of Vibrator social groups. The "Vibrator Club" was best known. For 44 years members regularly left for Northern Michigan in the fall and came back to hold great "game dinners." Berenice Lowe described club members parading on their return in 1877 with "48 deer besides wild geese, ducks, partridges and fish."

Fifty businesses closed for John Nichols' funeral in 1891, and his 350 employees marched in the procession. Edwin Nichols carried on the family traditions. He died in 1924,

Above: Longtime Oliver worker Max Chase shows blacksmith's skills at the forge. Hammer, tongs, and anvil were important to good craftsmanship even in the 20th century. Courtesy, Michigan Room, Willard Public Library

Right: Massive, power-driven "Red River Specials" required regular maintenance, but could be an awesome sight in operation. Early combines like this one proved successful on great bonanza farms in the west. Courtesy, Michigan Room, Willard Public Library

with an estate of $1.6 million, the largest the probate court had ever handled. Nichols recognized the importance of bonanza farming in the West and built the first of the company's "Red River Special" threshing machines in 1902. Other changes came as well. The first gasoline tractors rolled off the assembly line in 1912. The company continued to be a major employer through the 1920s, merging in 1929 with the Oliver Corporation and surviving the Depression. Defense contracts carried it during World War II, and it celebrated its centennial a few years later. Oliver sold its operation to White Motor Company in 1960.

Edwin Nichols presided as mayor over a major industrial city in 1880. Other firms, like Nichols & Shepard, combined management skills, product research, and shrewd marketing to build sales all over the country and abroad. They focused on what they did best and made their mark as well.

William Andrus reorganized the Battle Creek Table Company to keep it running in 1870. Two years later he sold his drugstore to become president of the Battle Creek Machinery Company, which he formed out of the implement factory Dorr Burnham began in 1854. The new firm concentrated on woodworking equipment and a "self-feeding wood sawing machine" shipped to successive lumber frontiers across the country. By the 20th century it was going strong as the American Marsh Pump Company.

Constantius Case worked for Nichols & Shepard until he developed an improved threshing machine himself. In 1881 he began making "The Advance" on his own. Andrus came forward again to put this firm on sound footing in 1883 and to see it move to large new quarters the same year. The Advance Threshing Machine Company continued in business until 1930.

By the end of the 1870s, Battle Creek bustled with activity. New factories and new business blocks shouldered each other downtown. Developers carved streets and building lots from pastureland around the edges of town. Seventy-three merchants together did more than a million dollars worth of business every year. While half the people in town kept a milk cow in 1850, now there were only 64 in all of the city.

By 1884 ten thousand fifty-one people lived in Battle Creek—twice as many families as the census taker found in 1870. Other changes came as well. The number of families matched the number of dwellings in 1870, but years later more than 400 families doubled up with others in "flats" or apartments. From the 1860s on, more women than men found opportunities in cities like Battle Creek. By 1884, however, heavy industry gave work to more men in Battle Creek and in most other industrial communities.

During the 1880s the city gained a variety of services. Telephones came in 1882, horse-drawn streetcars in 1883, and electric lights in 1884. City residents enjoyed running water brought from Goguac Lake by 1887. One observer announced with great pomp, "the solid prosperity of our city is due to the growth and success of our manufacturing institutions." Another argued that "Eastern culture and refinement, combined with Western energy and thrift" mattered most. A local reporter best described the transition from pioneer village to prosperous city when he called Battle Creek in 1889, "a city of beauty and of business, of culture and conscience, having voted the saloon a long vacation, and riding on four miles of street railway."

By the 1870s Battle Creek's businessmen worked in substantial brick buildings, though some, like J.M. Ward & Son, continued to use water power. Courtesy, Western Michigan University Archives

CHAPTER III

The Battle Creek Imprint

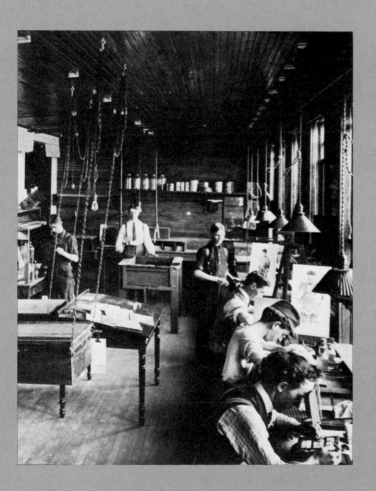

It was the end of the world—the Millenium—"Court Week in Heaven." In the early 1830s William Miller, an upper New York State farmer, had applied some esoteric mathematics to certain verses in the books of Daniel and Revelations, scrutinized recent world events, and concluded that Judgement Day was imminent. Sometime between March 21, 1843, and March 21, 1844, Miller's scenario ran, as Christ appeared in the sky, the righteous rose from the grave and the living righteous ascended heavenward, the world would be destroyed by fire. As Miller and his colleagues disseminated their fiery tracts and preached at revival meetings throughout New England and the frontier, thousands were converted.

The Millerites found fertile soil on the Michigan frontier. Elder Byron was an eccentric Methodist preacher from Climax, just west of the Calhoun County line. Once, when a convert asked to be baptized by pouring rather than sprinkling, Byron angrily dashed the whole contents of the vessel on him. Byron turned Millerite and traveled throughout the countryside foretelling "the speedy end of the world." Settlers traveled from near and far to hear Moses Clark preach the terrifying Millerite doctrines at the Methodist Meeting House in Climax. Daniel B. Eldred, a Battle Creek storekeeper, became so convinced that the world was ending that he ruined his business. Once, while en route to Kalamazoo, Eldred lost a linchpin from his wagon. A blacksmith in Galesburg made him a new pin but found it a little too large to fit readily. He was about to take it out and file it down when Eldred stopped him. "Drive it in," Eldred said, "it will answer for three days. I shan't want it after that, as the world is coming to an end." The smithy pounded the pin in "so tight that an ox-team could not have drawn it out," and Eldred continued on his way, proclaiming to all he met that "the end of the world is at hand."

As the final day approached, Millerites across the country prepared for the end. Women knit white cambric ascension robes, men abandoned their professions, left fields unplowed and crops unharvested, and children quit attending school. On Ascension Day, March 21, 1844, Miller's followers climbed nearby hills or gathered in cemeteries to watch the resurrection of their loved ones. The day following the "Great Disappointment" dawned on a sect somewhat embarrassed but still fast in their beliefs. Miller recalculated and established October 22, 1844, as the correct date for the Millenium. Once again fields lay fallow and chores neglected. Some Millerites grew hysterical, spoke in tongues, danced the holy dance, and laughed the holy laugh.

Many of Miller's followers took the second "Great Disappointment" of October 22, 1844, pretty hard. Some returned sheepishly to their run-down farms, others organized mobs, stormed meetinghouses, and held tar-and-feather parties. But not all Millerites abandoned their beliefs. A stubborn coterie worked out an explanation for the humiliation—Miller's computations were correct, but the error lay in his interpretation of what was to happen. One of these adamant believers was Ellen G. Harmon, a 17-year-old invalid living in Portland, Maine. A few months after the disappointment she began having strange visions. Shouting "Glory, Glory, Glory," she entered a trance-like state— arms flailing, unblinking eyes staring, breathless for up to six hours on end. She was in direct communication with the Lord, who showed her what to do and where to go. Out of the wreckage of the Millerite movement, augmented by the doctrine that Saturday ought to be celebrated as the Sabbath, and bolstered by the prophetic visions of a 17-year-old Maine farmgirl, grew the Seventh-Day Adventist Church.

Ellen Harmon soon took her visions on the road to become an evangelist. In 1846 she married another Adventist activist from Maine, James White, and together they toured New England and the West by train and wagon. They preached the fundamentalist doctrine that was evolving through James' and other church elders' interpretations and Ellen's visions. The printing press became an important ally to their proselytizing. In 1848 Sister White received a vision that directed her husband to begin publishing a denominational newspaper. He began a small paper at Middletown, Connecticut, in 1849 with barely enough money to pay the printer. By the autumn of 1850 the Whites had moved to Paris, Maine, where James published the first issue of an enlarged format, *The Second Advent Review and Sabbath Herald.* As the Whites

moved from place to place, preaching and printing, the paper followed, to Saratoga Springs, New York, in 1851 and Rochester in 1852. There the Adventists first acquired their own printing equipment, a Washington handpress.

The money needed to keep the newspapers and tracts flowing came largely through donations. Three Michigan Adventists stood in the forefront of the funding. Cyrenius Smith of Jackson, Henry Lyon of Plymouth, and James P. Kellogg of Tyrone each sold their farms worth about $3,500 and gave the money to the church. When the Whites toured Michigan in April 1855 they found considerable interest in their doctrines—particularly in Battle Creek. The local brethren raised $1,200 for a lot and structure and invited them to move the *Review* office to their city. The Whites accepted and soon installed the Washington press in a newly erected 20-by-30-foot, two-story wooden building on the southwest corner of West Main and Washington streets. On December 4, 1855, Battle Creek appeared on the masthead of the first number of the *Review* to be printed in an office owned by the Adventists.

Beyond financial inducements, other reasons may have motivated the Adventist exodus to Battle Creek. By 1855 the city had become a well-recognized haven for unorthodox creeds. Millerites-turned-Adventists remembered well the mobs and hot tar after the "Great Disappointment." Perhaps more importantly, a region that attracted strange attitudes and behaviors offered interesting challenges for a fundamentalist church.

Why Battle Creek developed a community exceptionally tolerant of the eccentric is somewhat of a mystery. Much the same mix of New Englanders and New Yorkers that pioneered most of southern Michigan settled in Calhoun County. Perhaps there was a bit more of an influx from the "burned-over district" of western New York State, the "psychic highway" that produced Jemima Wilkinson, the Fox sisters of spiritualist fame, and Joseph Smith and nurtured the Millerites and Adventists. Maybe Quaker pioneers, such as Underground Railroad conductor Erastus Hussey, seeded liberal tendencies. For whatever reason, there is no question that diverse and peculiar beliefs found a home in Battle Creek. When Ralph

THE PRESENT TRUTH.

PUBLISHED SEMI-MONTHLY—BY JAMES WHITE.

Vol.1.   MIDDLETOWN, CONN JULY, 1849.   No. 1.

" The secret of the Lord is with them that fear him; and he will shew them his covenant "—Ps. xxv. 14.

" WHEREFORE, I will not be negligent to put you always in remembrance of these things, though ye know them, and be established in the PRESENT TRUTH." 2 Pet. i: 12.

It is through the truth that souls are sanctified, and made ready to enter the everlasting kingdom. Obedience to the truth will kill us to this world, that we may be made alive, by faith in Jesus. "Sanctify them through thy truth; thy word is truth." John xvii: 17. This was the prayer of Jesus. "I have no greater joy than to hear that my children walk in truth." 3 John iv.

Error, darkens and fetters the mind, but the truth brings with it freedom, and gives light and life. True charity, or LOVE, "rejoiceth in the truth." Cor. xiii: 6. "Thy law is the truth." Ps. cxix: 142.

David describing the day of slaughter, when the pestilence shall walk in darkness, and destruction waste at noon-day, so that, "a thousand shall fall at thy side and ten thousand at thy right hand," says—

"He shall cover thee with his feathers, and under his wings shalt thou trust; his TRUTH shall be thy SHIELD and BUCKLER." Ps. xci: 4.

The storm is coming. War, famine and pestilence are already in the field of slaughter. Now is the time, the only time to seek a shelter in the truth of the living God.

In Peter's time there was present truth, or truth applicable to that present time. The Church have ever had a present truth. The present truth now, is that which shows present duty, and the right position for us who are about to witness the time of trouble, such as never was. Present truth must be oft repeated, even to those who are established in it. This was needful in the Apostles day, and it certainly is no less important for us who are living just before the close of time.

For months I have felt burdened with the duty of writing, and publishing the present truth for the scattered flock, but the way has not been opened for me to commence the work until now. I tremble at the word of the Lord, and the importance

of this time. What is done to spread the truth must be done quickly. The four Angels are holding the angry nations in check but a few days, until the saints are sealed, then the nations will rush, like the rushing of many waters. Then it will be too late to spread before precious souls, the present saving, living truths of the Holy Bible. My spirit is drawn out after the scattered remnant. May God help them to receive the truth, and be established in it. May they haste to take shelter beneath the "covering of Almighty God," is my prayer.

The Weekly Sabbath Instituted at Creation, and not at Sinai.

" And on the seventh day God ended his work which he had made; and he rested on the seventh day from all his work which he had made. And God blessed the seventh day, and sanctified it: because that in it he had rested from all his work which God created and made." Gen. ii: 2, 3.

Here God instituted the weekly rest or Sabbath. It was the seventh day. He BLESSED and SANCTIFIED that day of the week, and no other; therefore the seventh day, and no other day of the week is holy, sanctified time.

God has given the reason why he blessed and sanctified the seventh day. " Because that in it he had rested from all his work which God had created and made." He rested, and set the example for man. He blessed and set apart the seventh day for man to rest from his labor, and follow the example of his Creator. The Lord of the Sabbath said, Mark ii: 27 " The Sabbath was made for man." Not for the Jew only, but for MAN, in its broadest sense; meaning all mankind. The word man in this text, means the same as it does in the following texts. " Man that is born of a woman is of few days and full of trouble." Job xiv: 1. " Man lieth down and riseth not, till the heavens be no more." Job xiv: 12.

No one will say that man here means

Waldo Emerson lectured in the city in 1866 he discovered transplanted New Englanders "anxious for the success of radical politics," while pioneer historian Anson Van Buren noted in 1882 that Battle Creek had "ever been a place where 'isms' readily take root and flourish."

One of the first "isms" to arrive in the region, communism, sprang up in 1844 just west of Battle Creek on the banks of the Kalamazoo near Galesburg. Dr. Henry R. Schetterly convinced more than 300 area pioneers to participate in a religiously oriented Fourier socialist experiment called the Alphadelphia Society. The community built a tabernacle, a school, and a two-story, 20-by-200-foot mansion for dwelling, and published religious journals, *The Alphadelphia Tocsin* and *The Primitive Expounder*. By 1848 the society broke up for the usual reasons, or as one old pioneer remembered, there was "a hole in the meal bag from first to last."

The first half of the 19th century produced a

variety of curious religions that offered an alternative to the inflexibility of the traditional churches. Representatives of these avant-garde movements gravitated to Battle Creek. Followers of Emanuel Swedenborg organized a New Jerusalem Church sometime in the 1840s. The Swedenborgians believed that their prophet's teachings came via his direct communication with the spiritual world. The Quakers, outspoken antislavery activists, had appeared in Battle Creek in the 1830s but by the 1850s, after experimenting with spiritualism, eventually disbanded as a society. Anson Van Buren claimed that Battle Creek was the only town in the country where both a Swedenborgian and a Quaker church could be found. The Universalists, considered daring nonconformists in those doctrinally rigid days, established a church on Jefferson Street. Spiritualism, one of the most unusual creeds to arise in the 19th century, found a firm foothold in Battle Creek, which soon became "a sort of spiritualistic headquarters for the state."

Modern American spiritualism originated in 1848 in a small frame house located in the village of Hydesville, near Rochester, New York. The residents of the structure, the Fox

family, had been troubled for some time by mysterious sounds and occurrences. Margaretta and Catherine, teenage sisters, discovered they could communicate with the noisemaker, who rapped out answers to their questions. It seems he was the spirit of a 31-year-old peddler who had been murdered in the house for his money some five years previously. The ghost also knocked for neighbors and other witnesses. The Fox sisters moved to Rochester where they demonstrated their skills as mediums before large audiences. Before long the "Rochester rappers" had launched a religion that demonstrated that "there is no death." The very "city streets are thronged with an unseen people who flit about us, jostle us in thick crowds, and in our silent halls, our secret chambers, and our busiest haunts; their piercing eyes, invisible to us, are scanning all our ways." The Fox sisters had unlocked the secret that the universe teemed with spirits eager to communicate with the living via the "spiritual telegraph" of a sensitive medium. Soon interest in spiritualistic phenomena swept the country. Other individuals discovered that, like the Fox sisters, they had powers of occult communication, and Ouija boards, spirit slate writing, table

tippings, and seances became part of American popular culture.

While occasional spiritualist lecturers visited Battle Creek in the early 1850s, the movement's acceptance apparently began in the Quaker community. Warren Chase, "the lone one," a prominent spiritualist promoter, first visited Battle Creek in 1853 to deliver a course of lectures at the Quaker meetinghouse. He returned in 1855 to buy a lot and build a dwelling in the newly platted Quaker settlement of Harmonia, located six miles west of Battle Creek. The name Harmonia comes directly from spiritualist doctrine. Andrew Jackson Davis, "the Poughkeepsie Seer," originated the concept of harmonial philosophy through his *The Great Harmonia* and other works. At Harmonia, beginning in the early 1850s, Reynolds Cornell and his son, Hiram, operated a spiritualist-oriented academy conducted entirely by a staff of female teachers.

In 1857 the liberal community of Harmonia attracted the nationally known reformer, Sojourner Truth. She purchased a lot and resided there until moving to Battle Creek 10 years later. In 1850 Olive Gilbert published her biography, the *Narrative of Sojourner Truth*. As Sojourner lectured she sold copies of the volume to support herself. By 1860 a Battle Creek imprint graced the title page of Sojourner Truth's book.

Sojourner Truth apparently was not a spiritualist but settled among the Quakers of Harmonia because they also came from Ulster County, New York. Yet most other residents of Harmonia were somehow tied in with the movement. By 1858 spiritualism had become firmly entrenched in Battle Creek. Warren Chase assured his fellow spiritualists that the city was "the most lively and enterprising station between Detroit and Chicago, where our cause and friends are in the ascendant."

The Battle Creek cause gained a stalwart champion in 1856 when a gaunt giant of a man, dressed in black and sporting the long hair and beard of a biblical patriarch, rode down the city's dusty streets. James M. Peebles, "the spiritual pilgrim," had arrived to guide the local "rappers." Peebles grew up in western New York State in the 1820s where "he hated grindstones, axes, churns, and hoes." "His childhood ambition," wrote his biographer, J.O.

Elder James White, co-founder with his wife of the Seventh Day Adventist Church, appeared as a distinguished statesman in an 1878 steel engraving. James White died in Battle Creek in 1881. Courtesy, Duff Stoltz

Barrett, in 1871, "ran in the channel of the brooks, full of babbles and frolics," and he "gamboled with the minnows and owned all the butterflies and robins' eggs." In the early 1850s Peebles became a Universalist preacher. In 1856, while visiting Cleveland, he chanced to spend the night in a hotel room with the celebrated touring mediums, the Davenport brothers. After challenging them to do their stuff, Peebles retired. In the middle of the night the spirits rapped him awake, rocked his bed, knocked him around the room, and then informed him, "you are appointed for a great work; gird up your loins, buckle on your sandals, grasp the sword of truth. Go forth!" A few months later, the Reverend J.P. Averill, Universalist-turned-spiritualist, and Joseph Merritt and Eli Lapham, Quaker ministers, convinced Peebles to accept the pastorship of Battle Creek's "First Free Church."

Peebles found a receptive congregation at his new post, which he periodically augmented with converts. In 1858 Peebles assisted a traveling mesmerist in a demonstration of the hypnotic arts. One of the village rowdies and a particular thorn in Peebles' side sought to expose them both as a hoax. When the mesmerist put young Dunn into "magnetic sleep" on the stage, he suddenly went into convulsions, which Peebles recognized as "a species of trance peculiar to disorderly mediumship." Dunn's hand moved as if writing, and when given paper he scribbled what appeared as gibberish in "an unknown tongue." Peebles grabbed the manuscript, held it before a mirror, and read:

I was killed on the Great Western Railroad, near Hamilton, C.W., two hours ago. I have a wife and two children in Buffalo.

John Morgan

The following day's papers brought news of the accident and the death of John Morgan. Peebles garnered plenty of new believers, and Dunn, after apprenticeship under "the spiritual pilgrim," launched his own lucrative career as a traveling stage medium.

Peebles' platform experiences were not all successful, however. He branched into lecturing on morality and temperance and thundered to an audience in Decatur, Van Buren County,

"Let no man who swears come within four feet of me; six feet, who chews tobacco; ten feet, who drinks whiskey." A local judge, somewhat in his cups, teetered to the stage, proclaimed Peebles should be paid well for his eloquence, and pulled out a $10 gold piece. As Peebles reached out, the judge stepped back four feet and squealed, "I sometimes swear," stepping back six feet—"I chew tobacco," then back ten feet—"I drink whiskey," and put the half-eagle back in his pocket. The house roared at Peebles' expense.

For years Peebles had been sickly with consumption and other ailments, and the doctors pronounced him not long for this world. But one day, through the mediumship of an Albion woman, Peebles had the good fortune to contact the spirit of Chief Powhatan, of colonial Virginia fame. Powhatan developed a special fondness for Peebles, whom he nicknamed "Preach," and in pidgin English kept him posted on the Western Indian wars "four or five weeks ere the news appeared in the journals." Powhatan set about to cure "Preach" through his knowledge of secret herbal remedies. The chief guided the entranced Peebles to pick certain wild plants and to pound them into remedies, and even woke him at precise times of the night to quaff the mixtures. Soon Peebles was the picture of health. Every Fourth of July, the date Powhatan first revealed himself, Peebles celebrated by assembling local Potawatomies and whites for an oration in which he addressed the "pale faces" in English, and, through his mediumship, Powhatan exhorted his "red brethren" in their language.

Despite Powhatan's assistance, Peebles evidently found it hard to make ends meet. In 1860 he wandered off to California, El Dorado. During his absence Warren Chase, Benjamin Todd, Bell Scougal, and F.L. Wadsworth took over the spiritualist pulpit. But a year and a half later Peebles was back in Battle Creek. Finally, in the fall of 1867, he and his wife moved to New Jersey, "hoping for a more lucrative locality for a living."

Peebles turned to a literary career, cranking out "more volumes which have had a wider circle of readers than any other spiritual writer with the exception of A.J. Davis." The preface to his popular *Seers of the Ages* assured that "his trumpet has given no uncertain sound." His titles indicate his themes: *Who Are the Spiritualists and What is Spiritualism, The Christ Question Settled,* and *Hell Revised, Modernized and Made More Comfortable.* One of his spiritualist books reportedly sold 75,000 copies. Peebles also wrote on the subject of health reform, sharing his and, supposedly, Powhatan's unique theories in *Vaccination a Curse and a Menace to Personal Liberty.* His *How to Live a Century and Grow Old Gracefully* went through one edition of 20,000 copies. A passage from *Death Defeated, or the Psychic Secrets of How to Keep Young* illustrates Peebles' message and picturesque style:

Corsets are curses. They produce the wasp-like waist, and the wasp is both the meanest and most ill-

Above: *The smoldering ruins of the Battle Creek Adventist Tabernacle was a demoralizing sight in 1922. The "Tab" had been constructed in 1878 through dime contributions sent by Adventists from around the world. Courtesy, Michigan Room, Willard Public Library*

Left: *A lithographic view of the Review and Herald Printing Plant appeared in the 1877* Calhoun County History. *In 1878 a four-story central addition united the earlier Italianate structures under one roof. Approximately 100 employees operated seven presses to print millions of pages each year. Courtesy, Larry B. Massie*

shaped insect that lives. Had I the power, I would seize with a pair of tongs every corset on earth and making one great pyramid pile, and applying the torch, I would burn them to ashes and dance the highland-fling over their ashes. There young lady! now go and pout—and later repent, and reform, or die prematurely. If dying, let this be carved on your tombstone

"SUICIDED WITH THE CORSET."

While the citizenry of Battle Creek had temporarily lost the good services of "the spiritual pilgrim," the spiritualist movement there remained in good health. Warren Chase and others kept up the good work. Mrs. Alcinda W.

Slade from nearby Albion periodically lectured on spiritualism in Battle Creek. From Albion also, A.B. Whiting contributed such popular spiritualist tunes as "Waiting Only Waiting" and "Land of the So Called Dead." In March 1877 the special correspondent to the Niles (Michigan) *Democrat* reported from Battle Creek on the gala celebration of the 29th anniversary of modern spiritualism held at Stewart Hall. She acknowledged that the city "is the stronghold of Spiritualism, as it is of Adventism—the head center you might say." The festival drew speakers from across the country, including "some fifty celebrated mediums." Amidst colorful decorations, including large portraits of Thomas Paine and

Powhatan, the exercise opened with an invocation delivered under direct spirit influences followed by mediums speaking in "various unknown tongues." Unfortunately, observed the correspondent, a special large seance held during the evening failed because "conditions were not right." Beginning August 12, 1881, another mammoth celebration, the annual camp meeting of the state association of spiritualists, ran for 10 days on the shores of Goguac Lake.

Spiritualism was a potent force in 19th-century Calhoun County, but, of course, there were many who sought to discredit the movement as a hoax. While some might laugh at the table tippings and rapping, the Adventists did not doubt that the spiritualists were in communication with occult forces—with their prophetess periodically lapsing into a trance to receive divine instructions, how could they? However, Sister White's followers knew the spiritualists talked not to the dead but to devils. As long as spiritualism remained strong, the Adventists fought it tooth and nail. It seems probable that spiritualism's strength in Battle Creek provided another motive for the Adventist transfer there in 1855. Furthermore, their

mutual antipathy undoubtedly lent strength to both religions, as there is nothing like a worthy opponent to bring out the best.

Once in Battle Creek the Adventists flourished, as Anson Van Buren remembered, "like Jonah's gourd." Their first chapel, a 20-by-25-foot wooden structure erected in 1855 on the west side of Cass Street between Van Buren and Champion streets, accommodated a congregation of 40. Two years later they constructed a 30-by-45-foot building on the north side of Van Buren Street just west of Cass Street. A third larger church rose in 1868. Then in 1878 Adventists worldwide sent in dime contributions to finance the 3,000-seat "Dime Tabernacle." The "Tab" served as church as well as community center until fire destroyed it in 1922.

The Adventist printing plant grew at an even faster pace. The Whites fervently believed in the power of print as an aid to their evangelical mission. The little handpress they brought from Rochester could not satisfy their expectations. In 1857 twenty-five members of the denomination donated $100 each for the purchase of a modern Adams power press and a two-horsepower steam engine. Four years later the newly incorporated Seventh-Day Adventist Publishing Association replaced the original wooden office with a brick Italianate structure, two stories high and in the form of a Greek cross. Architecturally similar printing plants were constructed side by side on the corner of Main and Washington streets in 1871 and 1873. By 1878 a four-story central addition had united the structures built in 1861 and 1873, and rooflines had been remodeled in the popular mansard style.

Long before the breakfast cereal industry made Battle Creek a household phrase, the world knew the place name through the imprint on millions of books and periodicals. In 1878 one hundred employees ran seven large power presses to print thousands of books and periodicals with a monthly circulation of 40,000. The *Review* catalog listed 200 Battle Creek publications in English, 13 in French, 21 in Danish, 15 in Swedish, 13 in German, and one in Dutch. During the preceding two decades, more than 200 million pages of tracts had rolled off the Adventists' press. The Detroit *Post and Tribune* observed in 1878 that the

THE LITTLE HORN—SYMBOL OF THE PAPACY.

Left: *Uriah Smith's massive tome* Daniel and the Revelation, *published in Battle Creek in 1897, was a graphic rendition of the Adventist church's fierce antipapism. Such fanciful representations inspired millions to hew close to Adventist doctrine. Courtesy, Larry B. Massie*

Above: *Uriah Smith's* Our Country: Its Past, Present, and Future, *published by the Review and Herald Press in 1886, contains a double-page lithograph idealizing American progress. An embodiment of American manifest destiny carries the Bible while stringing telegraph lines across the continent. Meanwhile the Indians are pushed westward by American expansion. Courtesy, Larry B. Massie*

church operated "by all odds the most complete and largest publishing house in Michigan." By 1881 the volume of mail generated by the *Review* publishers placed Battle Creek, with a population of only 7,500, among the top three Michigan post offices.

A decade and a half later 262 employees—typesetters, pressmen, foundrymen, engravers, electrotypers, and proofreaders—converted more than two million pounds of paper each year into a torrent of print that reached more than 20 nations. Every day but Saturday the Adventist bindery bound 5,000 volumes. In 1902, with 80,000 square feet of floor space, the Review and Herald Press pronounced itself Polyglot Printers, "the largest printing establishment between Buffalo and Chicago."

Suddenly, on December 30 of that year, there was a flash of light, a muffled explosion, and fire raced through the huge printing plant. Firemen's efforts in the bitterly cold weather served only to coat Washington Avenue with a glaze of ice on which children merrily slid. Fueled by

tons of paper and ink-soaked floors, the flames leveled the brick-veneered wooden building. Mother Ellen White, disenchanted by what she considered the city's evil ways, had pronounced, a "sword of fire hung over Battle Creek." Fire had struck eight other Adventist-related structures during the previous decade, but the Review and Herald conflagration was the biggest loss.

The Adventist Church began pulling out of the city that had been its headquarters for nearly half a century. In 1902 the Adventist college left Battle Creek for Berrien Springs. The following year the General Conference headquarters and the Review and Herald Press relocated in the Washington, D.C., suburb of Tacoma Park. The Review and Herald Press, the Pacific Press Publishing Company in Mountain View, California, and various foreign printing establishments continued to pour out denominational works. But the famous Battle Creek imprint no longer appeared on Adventist literature. In 1946 workmen erased the last vestige of the city's Adventist publishing history when they razed the plant constructed in 1873 on the southwest corner of West Michigan and Washington avenues to make way for a new gas station.

Yet thousands of books bearing the Battle Creek imprint survive as treasured relics of the city's golden age of printing. Beyond their artifactual value, these Battle Creek imprints document the evolution of a significant American religion. Ellen White's *Testimonials*, amalgams of her interpretations of the scriptures, general observations on the conduct of the flock, and her visions comprise one of the more important sources. Returning from a divine interview, limp and pale, Sister White would dash off a testimonial, which before being set in type sometimes received the benefit of Elder White's editorial assistance. The testimonials, originally dressed in paper wraps, often contained harsh criticisms of doctrinal and behavioral errors. When the unruly needed humbling, Sister White did not mince words. In a 53-page pamphlet published in 1872, *The Health Reform and the Health Institute,* she paused to chastise an unfortunate Health Institute staff member:

Irwin Royce is not what God would have him be. He has an exalted opinion of himself. He talks too much. He does not have a humble mind. Sometimes he talks in an unbecoming manner to patients. This would be wrong were he even superintendent of the Institution, but in the position as a common helper, he should be the last one to dictate to patients, or to speak to them disrespectfully. . . . The time that Irwin spends in chatting with the helpers, can be better employed. He is too set in his own way, and he needs to cultivate humility.

Later editions of the *Testimonials* replaced names with dashes and eliminated or bowdlerized certain passages.

Traditionally Adventist churches operated without the aid of a resident preacher, although they were periodically visited by itinerants. This permitted the professional ministers to devote most of their time to proselytizing and to writing. In what became perhaps the original doctrine of "publish or perish," Adventist elders churned out enormous quantities of verbiage. One of the earliest large tracts to be printed in Battle Creek appeared in 1860, Elder J.H. Waggoner's diatribe against the hated spiritualists, *The Nature and Tendency of Modern Spiritualism.* Soon the Adventists produced more ambitious and professional appearing volumes. In 1862 the Review and Herald Press printed an edition of J.N. Andrews' *History of the Sabbath* and sent it back to Rochester for a suitable cloth binding. Andrews wielded the pen with such might that Immanuel Mission-

ary College, the Adventist seminary in Berrien Springs, was renamed Andrews University in his honor. Other leading literary elders of the early period included Joseph Bates, W.H. Littlejohn, J.N. Loughborough, and James White himself.

Uriah Smith was probably the most prolific of the ilk. A native of New Hampshire, Smith had been converted to Adventism in 1852 and joined James White on the staff of the Review and Herald a year later. When the press moved to Battle Creek, he followed and for nearly half a century wrote diligently for the Adventist cause. He also dabbled in secular affairs to publish *Key to Smith's Diagram of Parliamentary Rules,* a type of Robert's *Rules of Order.* Somewhat of an inventor, Smith patented a pioneer mechanical leg to replace the one he lost as a child, a cane that converted into a stool, and a novel school seat that automatically lowered into place when sat on and folded up when not in use. He constructed a factory to manufacture his "automatic seats," but he later sold out at a handsome profit.

Throughout the 19th century Adventist writers devoted plenty of text to an analysis of contemporary happenings. They were not about to make William Miller's mistake in predicting the exact date of the Millenium, but periodically, as they applied their apocalyptical talents to certain world developments, it certainly seemed that the signs of the times pointed toward the big event. Uriah Smith's *The Marvel of Nations, Our Country: Its Past, Present and Future . . .* (Battle Creek, 1886) offered an Adventist interpretation of American history. Smith attached special significance to contemporary attempts to legally prosecute those who labored on Sunday, which the Adventists saw as an attempt to mingle church and state—a bad portent. A decade later Smith's *Daniel and the Revelation* (Battle Creek, 1897), a huge tome that sold 77,000 copies the first year of publication, exhaustively treated the same topic. The elder singled out the Roman Catholic Church, which, in a curiously convoluted logic, he saw as the "beast" of the prophecies intent on evil ends via civil power. The fierce anti-papistry found in much of the Adventist literature reached massive proportions in Alonzo T. Jones' 895-page treatise, *The Two Republics or Rome and the United States of America* (Battle

Creek, 1891). By the turn of the century James E. White's *The Coming King* (Battle Creek, 1900) linked the labor unrest of the 1890s, the Boer War, and the Spanish American War as signs of the Second Coming.

Occasionally, however, the church had occasion to regret the literary output of its followers. Moses Hull wrote for the *Review* from 1861 to 1864. He hewed close to the doctrinal line with tracts such as *The Bible from Heaven...* (Battle Creek, 1863), *The Two Laws and the Two Covenants* (Battle Creek, 1862), and *Infidelity and Spiritualism* (Battle Creek, 1862). Evidently he got to mulling over the latter subject too much, for, to the embarrassment of the church, he left Battle Creek in 1864 to become a confirmed spiritualist. He plied his pen in support of his new religion to contribute such interesting titles as *Jesus and the Mediums, Joan: The Medium,* and *All About Devils.*

Periodically, defection of another elder jolted the church hierarchy. One who apostatized in a big way was Elder D.M. Canright. After 28 years as an Adventist and a career as a highly touted lecturer and author, Canright left in 1887 to become a Baptist. If that was not enough, from his home in Otsego he poured forth a torrent of anti-Adventist tracts. In 1888 he published in Kalamazoo, certainly not Battle Creek, *Seventh-Day Adventism Renounced*. "The proof is abundant," Canright observed, "that Mrs. White's visions are merely the result of nervous disease, a complication of hysteria, catalepsy, and ecstacy." Ecstasy could not describe Sister White's reaction to Canright's book, but as is usually the case, criticism only made the church grow stronger.

By the turn of the century the circulation of Adventist publications had reached enormous figures. According to contemporary advertisement, the 128-page children's book, *The Gospel Primer,* sold 400,000 copies. The Adventists distributed their literature in a variety of ways. Prior to 1853 all publications were given away, with donations helping to defray printing expenses. But times were tough, and by 1854 White advertised an annual subscription rate of one dollar for the *Review*. In July of that year the Adventists first tried to sell their tracts at a tent meeting in McComb County, Michigan, and, to their surprise, sold $50 worth. White wrote jubilantly in the *Review*, "This shows that our books can be sold." In 1857 the first financial report noted book receipts of $1,287.91 over the preceding two years. That was just the beginning.

Mail delivery soon supplemented hawking books at camp meetings as a sales technique. Advertisements in Adventist journals listed titles and prices. Later, readers found more complete catalogs bound into the rear of volumes. By 1877 dozens of works, ranging from denominational treatises, hymn books, and small tracts to health reform publications, were available at prices ranging from half a cent for leaflets to a dollar and a half for large bound volumes.

Following the Civil War, an army of unemployed veterans popularized the technique of door-to-door book sales. Canvassers, armed with a heavily illustrated prospectus containing examples of various binding styles, testimonials, and blank sheets for ordering, incessantly hounded householders and businessmen. Throughout the remainder of the 19th century subscription book selling became

The Gage Printing Company produced Thomas N. Doutney's autobiography in 1891. The volume traces Doutney's early life as a drunkard, his later salvation, and eventual career as a temperance lecturer. Here the youthful Doutney receives an object lesson from a New York City bartender. Courtesy, Larry B. Massie

Above: *W.J. Fairfield drew a series of pictures exhibiting the effects of alcoholism to accompany his poetical rendition,* The Man That Rum Made, *published in Battle Creek in 1886. Courtesy, Larry B. Massie*

Right: *Battle Creek's Gage Printing Company won turn-of-the-century renown as a publisher of fine promotional and catalog work. Gage produced a catalog for the local American Steam Pump Company with excellent typography, circa 1900. Courtesy, Larry B. Massie*

a dominant method of merchandising popular volumes.

In January 1878 *The Health Reformer* sought 500 canvassers to solicit orders. To sweeten the pitch, a free copy of John Harvey Kellogg's *Household Manual*, a compendium of recipes and medical information, was given away with every $1.25 subscription. For one dollar prospective salesmen got the "canvasser's outfit" containing specimen copies of *The Health Reformer* and order forms. The following year Sister White timely received her first vision concerning the colporteur work. After she produced a "testimony" indicating that it was good to sell books door-to-door, Adventists began canvassing in earnest. Their first subscription book, Uriah Smith's *Thoughts on Daniel and the Revelation* (Battle Creek, 1882), was followed by scores of others, each available in a binding style to suit diverse tastes and pocketbooks. Ellen White's own *The Desire of Ages*, an 866-page life of Christ, became available only through subscription at $2.50 for the "popular edition, plain edges," $4.25 for gilt edges, and $7 for a full morocco binding. By 1895 the Adventists could report book sales of $5 million over the previous decade.

While the vast majority of publications bearing the Review and Herald imprint were sectarian in nature, to keep the presses running between visions and to make extra income, the Adventists took on job printing. Local historian Anson Van Buren's *Jottings from the South* (Battle Creek, 1859), an account of his pedagogical tour of the slave states, became the first commercial publication. In 1888 the Adventist press published the third edition of Colonel George Hunter's *Reminiscences of an Old Timer*, describing his pioneering adventures in the Pacific Northwest. Other job-printed works like Detroit lawyer and Prohibition activist Charles Sedgwick May's *Speeches of the Stump, the Bar, and the Platform* (Battle Creek, 1899) may have appealed to the Adventists from a philosophical basis. By the late 1890s the Review and Herald Press actively solicited catalog and journal printing. At that time it printed the *Bay View Magazine*, the organ of Michigan's Methodist-derived counterpart to the Chautauqua home-education movement.

Periodically, dissenting voices among church leadership challenged the policy of publishing

EDWARD C. HINMAN, President   LEOPOLD WERSTEIN, Vice-President
RICHARD R. HICKS, Secretary
FOSTER M. METCALF, Mechanical Engineer

▼ CATALOGUE ▼
NUMBER 18

MARSH & AMERICAN STEAM & POWER PUMPING MACHINERY

ASK THE MAN WHO RUNS ONE

Marsh Steam Pumps & Air Compressors.
American Simple & Compound Pumps.
American Power Pumps & Air Compressors

▼

AMERICAN STEAM PUMP COMPANY
MAIN OFFICES AND WORKS
BATTLE CREEK, MICHIGAN, U.S.A.

non-Adventist works. During the early 1880s the Review and Herald Press temporarily decided to abandon the field of commercial printing. The prospect of picking up business refused by the church led two Review and Herald pressmen to embark on their own venture. Cornelius De Vos had learned the printing trade in the early 1870s in Iowa, became interested in Adventism, and joined the staff of the Review and Herald Press in 1878. In 1883 De Vos and his brother, John, formed their own job-printing establishment, De Vos Brothers. Eight months later, William C. Gage, a master printer from Manchester, New Hampshire, who had worked with the De Voses at the Review and Herald Press, joined them. Gage, De Vos & Company operated out of a little office on West Main Street. The De Vos brothers left in 1884, later to return. In the interim Gage and his sons Fred W. and Frank H. organized Wm. C. Gage & Sons, Printers.

In 1890 Gage constructed a four-story plant on the corner of McCamly and West State streets. By the turn of the century, the Gage Printing Company had become one of only a few printing establishments in the United States that accomplished all its own production work under one roof. Fifty skilled workers wrote copy, photographed goods, designed and engraved plates, engraved etchings, set type, electrotyped plates, performed presswork, and bound the printed sheets. The Gage Company specialized in illustrated catalogs. Two of the products executed for Battle Creek firms, an American Steam Pump Company catalog from 1900 and the Postum Cereal Company's promotional booklet, *There's a Reason*, circa 1914, represent prime examples of the printer's art. With the development of the local breakfast food industry, the Gage Company diversified into the printing of colorful cereal cartons. Occasionally the Gage Company executed full-scale volumes. In 1891 it printed and bound *Thomas N. Doutney: His Life Struggle, Fall, and Reformation*. A vivid pictorial cover, lurid illustrations, and 544 pages of text document the usual story of a reformed tosspot turned temperance lecturer.

Doutney led his life of drunkenness out East, but undoubtedly his biography sold well in the city where it was printed. Battle Creek enjoyed a long tradition of temperance reform. From their arrival the Adventists had railed against spirits as well as spiritualists. In February 1877 Dr. Henry A. Reynolds stormed into Battle Creek to organize a Red Ribbon Club. Tipplers took the pledge against alcohol and then spent their time spying on backsliding members. Reynolds appealed to local imbibers through his own confessions:

I am one of the unfortunate men who inherited an appetite for strong drink. I love liquor as well as a baby loves milk. When I was but a child of less than eight years of age I began to strengthen that appetite first by drinking cider. Cider I call the devil's kindling-wood. Next I used to drink native wines, then ale and lager bier, and the stronger drinks. I drank at parties, weddings, dances . . .

In 1886 another Battle Creek publisher, the J.E. White Company, produced a book for a juvenile audience that traced a similar path of degradation. A local doctor, W.J. Fairfield, penned the poetical tract for the "children of drunkards." Fairfield, also president of the Battle Creek Art Club, endowed the volume with colorful graphics that plotted the metamorphosis of *The Man that Rum Made*.

This is the eye, all bleared and awry
Surmounting the cheek, so flabby and weak,
By the side of the nose that blossoms and grows
On the face of the man that rum made.

Other Battle Creek entrepreneurs turned to book publishing to address various needs of the 1880s. Corodon S. Cannon produced *Cannon's Universal Proof of Money Making or Business Cyclopedia* in 1880. Cannon humbly described his handiwork as "the only real work ever pub-

A small array of newsboys gathered for a group photograph in front of the Battle Creek Enquirer and Evening News *in 1913. The newspaper office was located at North McCamly Street near State Street. Courtesy, Michigan Room, Willard Public Library*

In 1888, the corner of Main and Division streets was jammed as hundreds of Battle Creek residents turned out to watch the Labor Day parade. The horse-drawn streetcar line began in 1882. Courtesy, Michigan Room, Willard Public Library

master, P.R. Spencer, also drew full-page plates of elaborate Spencerian handwriting specimens. S.S. Hulbert and F.R. Mechem, Battle Creek lawyers, furnished a chapter on commercial law. Professor C.W. Stone, principal of the Battle Creek Business College, dealt with the subject of correspondence by providing a variety of model letters. The Honorable W.C. Gage, ex-mayor who would soon establish his own publishing firm, wrote on etiquette. Uriah Smith added his system of parliamentary practice.

Subscription agents armed with copies of the prospectus and the motto "knowledge is power" fanned out across the country. The undertaking met with unusual success. One colporteur wrote from Missouri, "I am an experienced canvasser, but never saw a book sell like *Parsons' Hand Book*. Put 600 books in one county. Put 90 in one township that registered only 150 voters. Put 18 books into 18 consecutive houses, on one road in the country." Subscribers might order the thick volume in bindings ranging from plain or pebbled cloth, calf or morocco at four to six dollars a copy—a hefty price for a book in the 1880s. *Parsons' Hand Book* ran through five editions of more than 50,000 copies in less than two years.

While thousands learned business acumen by studying *Parsons' Hand Book* at home, others traveled to Parsons' Business College in Kalamazoo for a more formal education. By the early 20th century students studied textbooks bearing the institution's motto "learn to do by doing" as well as the imprint of another famous Battle Creek firm, the Ellis Publishing Company. In 1886 two staff members of Eureka College in Eureka, California, Neil S. Phelps and Charles L. Ellis, formed a company to publish a system of business education training aids developed by Ellis. Following a visit to Battle Creek in 1893 during which Ellis met a local job printer, Hiram Williams, they relocated to a small frame building on West Main Street. The Ellis Publishing Company began printing educational journals, commercial school textbooks, and other school supplies. As the enterprise grew, they erected a three-story plant across the Battle Creek on Canal Street. The local YMCA staged a month-long carnival to celebrate its grand opening in 1899. At that time Ellis Publishing printed a heterogeneous

lished of its kind or nature, and must serve as a great pilot and benefactor to lead thousands, yea, millions, from poverty and oppression into greater ease, luxury, and even opulence, gaining more freedom, whether on land or on water, in the old world or the new." The volume's 355 pages of close-set type in reality contained nothing more than a heterogeneous hodgepodge of articles Cannon had clipped from several years of newspapers. The publisher "offered extra inducements to agents in every township" to sell his volume at $1.25 in paper and $1.60 bound in half leather. Cannon's ultimate "proof of money making" came not through perusal of his book but by the example of his success in selling the worthless compilation.

A business guide that did better by its purchasers, *Parsons' Hand Book of Business and Social Forms*, appeared in 1882. The successful subscription publisher and son of Elder and Sister White, James Edson White, of 5 West Main Street, put out this 700-page encyclopedia of practical information. The volume, he promised, "excluded all frivolous or unimportant matter." White secured a variety of distinguished local talent to collaborate on his business guide. Professor William E. Parsons, founder of Parsons' Business College in Kalamazoo, lent his name to the venture and contributed chapters on bookkeeping and penmanship. Parsons, who had studied under the

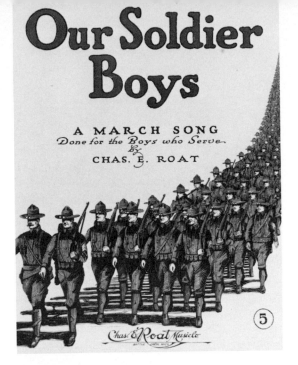

Our Soldier Boys

A MARCH SONG
Done for the Boys who Serve
by
CHAS. E. ROAT

⑤

Chas E Roat Music

variety of materials. Their lavishly illustrated sets, such as John L. Stoddard's *Lectures* and Burton Holmes' *Travel Lectures*, brought the wonders of world travel into thousands of Victorian homes, while vanity press poetical works like J.W. Bryce's *Random Rhymes* (Battle Creek, 1899), which contained "Apostrophe to Goguac," described local scenery.

> *Hail thou, gentle Goguac,*
> *That nestles 'mongst the hills*
> *Where piping note of songbird*
> *The air with music fills*
> *Where monarchs of the forest*
> *In all their verdure green,*
> *Maintain in regal splendor*
> *A majesty serene . . .*

In 1940 the Ellis Company withdrew from the publishing business to specialize in job printing. The city acquired the plant over the stream in 1953 and razed it to make way for a parking lot. When Ellis constructed his modern new plant in 1899, few would have suspected that Battle Creek would ever require a parking lot for automobiles. Life was simpler then, less hectic, and people found time to read more. A person could keep posted on almost any subject, in fact, by consulting a local publication. Battle Creek ranked third in the state in the number of newspapers, magazines, and periodicals published. Two dailies, eight weeklies, fourteen monthlies, and two quarterlies conveyed information on religion, health and hygiene, medicine, temperance, education, literature, and game cocks. And admirers of man's best friend knew Battle Creek through the imprint on the only two exclusively dog-oriented journals then published — *Dogdom* and

The Dog Fancier. The Dogdom Publishing Company also produced a variety of related monographs, such as Edward Axtell's *The Boston Terrier and All About It* (Battle Creek, 1910).

The turn-of-the-century heyday of Battle Creek printing saw the beginnings of another publisher that catered to a specialized trade, the Charles E. Roat Music Company. During the 1890s Charles Roat, a clerk at the Nichols & Shepard threshing machine works, began a mail-order business selling sheet music. In 1897 he published his own piece, "Company D Waltzes." Roat finally quit his job at the plant in 1902 to publish music full time. For 20 years he quietly operated from his office at 60 West Michigan Avenue and barely made ends meet. His struggle ended in 1922 when he bought a song called "Faded Love Letters" from some Detroit writers. The tune swept the nation, selling more than 200,000 copies, and Roat became a success. He followed that hit with one of his own compositions, "Pal of My Dreams," which sold a quarter of a million copies. When Roat died in 1936, many Americans still hummed his catchy songs.

"It may be safely said," boasted a local turn-of-the-century promotional piece, "that no other city in the United States of the size of Battle Creek is so extensively engaged in the printing and publishing industry." Yet the printing presses that stamped Battle Creek on millions of books and journals to promote that name worldwide vied with another industry that loomed equally large in the annals of the city's commercial history — the business of health.

Left: Battle Creek sheet music publisher Charles E. Roat produced a patriotic march in 1917. Not until 1922 did Roat print a nationally popular tune: "Faded Love Letters." Courtesy, Michigan Room, Willard Public Library

Below: Battle Creek's electric streetcars replaced the earlier horse-drawn cars in 1891 and operated until 1932. The Maple car, shown here circa 1910, carried thousands of downtown passengers to Goguac Lake. Courtesy, Michigan Room, Willard Public Library

CHAPTER IV

The Business of Health

By the final quarter of the 19th century, the trains that puffed out of Battle Creek laden with examples of the printer's art also conveyed increasing numbers of sickly passengers. The "Queen City" had become a mecca for the run-down and worn-out practitioners of unhealthy living. Shaking with ague, wheezing with catarrh, or doubled up with dyspepsia, they sought rejuvenation through a vigorous health-oriented industry. As with the printing trade, the business of health sprang from the Adventist Church.

The antebellum decades that gave rise to the golden age of reform in America—movements promoting abolition, women's rights, temperance, and new religions—spawned a full complement of health reform theories as well. Russell Trall and Joel Shew popularized hydropathy, a water cure discovered by a Silesian peasant. Sylvester Graham, who left the graham cracker as a legacy, and other members of the American Vegetarian Society preached their distinctive dietary doctrines. Orson Fowler designed octagon houses for healthier living and taught that bumps on the head revealed a person's character. Fowler teamed up with another phrenologist, Samuel Wells, to establish a New York publishing house that broadcast volumes promoting these novel theories. The root of the problem, most of the health reformers agreed, lay in Americans' tendency "to fill their mouths with pork, rum, and tobacco."

In the 1850s Dr. James Caleb Jackson converted a run-down hotel near Dansville in western New York State into "Our Home on the Hillside," a health spa that incorporated most of the progressive cures of the era. Dr. Horatio Lay, an Adventist, checked his sickly wife into the "home" in the early 1860s. Impressed with the results, he joined the institution as a staff member. His recommendations induced a number of other run-down Adventists to sample the Dansville regimen. Elder and Sister White arrived in 1865 and found the setup much to their liking.

Adventist dogma had been moving toward the union of spiritual and health reform for some time. Since the Millerite days the church had decried alcoholic beverages. In 1863 at an Otsego, Michigan, farmhouse Sister White received her first divine communication concerning diet reform—two meals a day and no meat. Following her visit to Jackson's spa she had a vision that directed the church to establish a similar institution in Battle Creek. Dr. Lay resigned at Dansville and by the fall of 1866 had transformed a small two-story farmhouse located on a seven-acre tract just west of the city limits into the Western Health Reform Institute.

The Adventists sunk a good deep well and erected a windmill and a 300-gallon water tank to accommodate the hydropathic regimen. By 1868 the Institute could advertise that "people are continually coming here very low with disease and after going through with a course of treatment go away well." Patients received no drugs; instead they exercised, sat in tubs of water, dined twice a day on saltless vegetarian fare prepared in a kitchen where "grease and spice took a back seat," and, in lieu of the companionship of alcohol, tobacco, tea, and coffee, got plenty of cold water inside and out. Hard graham biscuits and crackers comprised a staple item on the menu. Soon the Battle Creek City Bakery announced that it was prepared to furnish graham flour at seven dollars a barrel and graham crackers at eight cents a pound for home consumption.

The year the Adventists opened the Institute they also launched a periodical to circulate their newly acquired precepts, *The Health Reformer*. Dr. Russell Trall contributed a medical column to promote his distinctive theories. Trall stressed the significance of the alimentary canal. "Three-fourths of all pulmonary and nasal difficulties that are attributed to the weather and climate, are really caused by overeating," he wrote in 1868. A sufferer from heart trouble learned that the cause of his complaint was constipation. Some topics have a modern ring to them. "Has any person the right to poison the air?" wrote an indignant nonsmoker, who found the atmosphere in public places "poisoned with the stench of tobacco smoke or the poisonous breath of some tobacco-sot." Articles by Trall and numerous correspondents exposed the evils of salt pork, pickles, hard cider, and tight lacing.

Ladies' fashion reform had also become an item of Adventist dogma. Sister White first delicately approached the subject in the early 1860s when she wrote, "women should wear their dresses so as to clear the filth of the street an inch or two." Following her visit to Dansville, where she was exposed to the short skirt and pantaloon ensemble popularized by Amelia Bloomer, Sister White went into vision to learn that the reform dress was "in" for Adventists. Nine inches from the ground was the new Battle Creek look. Sister White presented a battery of reasons in support of the shortened skirt. Long dresses "swept up the dirt and mud and licked up tobacco spittle and all manner of filth" from the streets, women stumbled on their own skirts, and careless gentlemen trod on and ripped them. Those who thought Bloomers immoral had evidently not, like Sister White, observed "exposed forms" as women raised their long skirts to mount steps.

In the summer of 1868 when Dr. Trall arrived in Battle Creek to deliver a course of lectures, he "had the pleasure of seeing nearly 300 women in the short dress." Trall noted that the style had become so common "that it ceased to attract any special attention on the streets." Sister White would not have rated the experience as successful. An extremely embarrassing coincidence had occurred. Local spiritualists also adopted a similar outfit en masse. "Frequently," Sister White lamented, "strangers would ask, 'Are you spiritualists?'" One can imagine her apoplectic reaction. A "sense of duty" led the Adventists to "bear the cross of the reform dress" for about eight years. Then they quietly returned to normal styles.

Periodically the Adventists experimented with other health-related apparel. In 1874 advertisements in the *The Health Reformer* promoted novel "skirt supports," which held up the dress like a pair of suspenders. Rather incongruously, in 1877, on the same page that the journal announced a new Adventist tract, *The Evils of Fashionable Dress*, it ran an advertisement for the sensational "adjustable cork bosom pad," whose perfect shape was both healthy and graceful. By 1902 the dress department of *Good Health*, successor to *The Health Reformer*, promoted the "Good Health adjustable waist," which laced up very much like a corset to produce the desired hourglass figure.

In addition to the usual contingent of homeopathic, allopathic, and eclectic doctors, the budding Western Health Reform Institute competed with other interesting Calhoun County practitioners. At his Medical Depot located on Superior Street in Albion, Dr. J.D. Maxson combined the "German, eclectic, and hydropathic schools." Maxson specialized in "persons that had been given up to die under other treatments" who were "frequently raised to health" through his new system of medicine. For those who could not make it into the Depot for treatment, Maxson published a *Guide to Health* in 1862. Dr. Maxson did not believe in making fine distinctions. "The same cause that produces one kind of fever produces them all," he wrote, consequently, "the same treatment that will cure one kind of fever will cure them all." At the onset of any illness, Maxson advised, "take a handful each of Wahoo, Cher-

In 1866 the Adventist Church purchased the Benjamin Graves homestead and converted it into the Western Health Reform Institute, a hydropathic and dietary cure institution patterned after Dr. James Caleb Jackson's "Our Home on the Hillside" in Dansville, New York. Courtesy, Michigan Room, Willard Public Library

ry, Popple, and Prickly Ash barks, Golden Seal, Bloodroot, Liferoot, Wandering Milkweed, and Culver root, and put them in a gallon of whiskey and take a swallow three times a day, in addition to bathing, and a person will soon feel all right again." For snakebite he recommended doses of his special "Detergent syrup" or "to drink freely of whiskey or brandy." "Take a large drink every half hour," he prescribed, "until you become a little intoxicated. Sometimes it takes a quart of whiskey to do it."

Dr. A.S. Johnson held forth at his Medical Dispensary located in the Centennial Block of downtown Battle Creek. Since 1868 Johnson had specialized in all diseases of the throat and lungs and of a private nature. He offered partic-

ular attention to "young men suffering from the effects of such youthful indiscretions" as "the solitary vice." "Never use patent medicines nor let any one experiment upon you, but come or send at once to the Doctor, who understands these diseases," Johnson urged. His armamentarium consisted of his own carefully concocted nostrums, including: Dr. Johnson Female Elixir, Constipation Powders, Consumption Cure, Malarial Antidote, Blood Purifier, Dyspepsia Pills, and his leader, Dr. Johnson's Preventive to Venereal Disease, which he put up in dollar bottles. In 1879 Johnson directed anyone desiring references concerning his medical sanding to "communicate with any of the businessmen of Battle Creek."

The lucrative health business inspired assorted imaginative adversaries. Dr. Dye from Marshall manufactured a "Voltaic Belt" that restored lost manhood. Mrs. Ellen Overholt, a Battle Creek "electrician," shocked her patients back to health. Mrs. M.E. Pendill, "the celebrated Indian Doctress," operated out of an office at the Swedish Movement Cure. She offered this rationale for her services: "Men never have and never can understand a woman in health, why should you trust them in sickness?" And a number of traveling clairvoyants descended on the city to provide remedies direct from the hereafter. The Western Health Reform Institute's ascetic life-style and cold baths lacked flamboyance. Sister White's charisma was fine for the spiritual realm, but even her far-ranging visions dared not venture into the internal workings of the body. By the mid-1870s the Health Reform Institute floundered with about a dozen guests. The Adventists needed a showman who was also a respectable medical doctor to promote their regimen and to get more paying customers grinding away at their graham biscuits.

The man who combined those traits, and who would salvage the operation and build it into an organization beyond the Whites' wildest expectations, was John Harvey Kellogg. Kellogg, one of 16 offspring sired by Adventist stalwart John Preston Kellogg, was born in Tyrone, Michigan, in 1852. A half-century before the Kellogg name came to be linked with cornflakes, it stood for corn brooms. The elder Kellogg established the first broom factory west

Left: *Sister White's version of the daring "Bloomer" outfit appeared in* The Health Reformer *in 1868. While extremely modest by modern standards, the fashion was considered scandalous by contemporary Battle Creek residents. Courtesy, Larry B. Massie*

writing popular health guides. While still a student Kellogg had published his first book in 1874, *The Proper Diet for Man,* and following graduation, his second, *The Use of Water in Health and Disease.* However, in 1876 he took over editorship of the *The Health Reformer* and, before the year was over, had been persuaded to return to Battle Creek to replace Dr. William Russell as superintendent of the Health Institute.

The dynamic five-foot, three-inch doctor set to work with a flourish. He coined a colorful name for the Institute, the Battle Creek Sanitarium, changed the name of *The Health Reformer* to *Good Health,* launched a building campaign, and supplemented the water cure regimen with more scientific procedures. Within two years a huge, four-story mansard building, wrapped with 600 feet of veranda, stood amidst 20 acres of "groves, lawns, walks and croquet grounds." In 1877 V.C. Smith, who had just sampled the new regimen, thought the Sanitarium "destined to wield a mighty influence in the world, and to be a powerful means of breaking down the old pernicious autocracy of empirical medical practice." By 1881 eighty doctors, nurses, cooks, masseurs, and bath attendants catered to 350-400 paying patients. Kellogg found time during his reorganization of the Sanitarium to write.

of Detroit in the 1850s. Young Kellogg left school at the age of 10 to work for his father. When he was 12 Kellogg started as a printer's devil at the *Review and Herald* office. Three years later he had worked up to the editorial department, and by the time he was 16, he edited the entire journal.

In true Adventist tradition Kellogg had experienced a vision at the age of 10 that outlined his life's work—he would become a doctor. The Whites agreed to help finance Kellogg's medical education, and he went first to the State Normal at Ypsilanti, then to the University of Michigan. He transferred to Bellevue Hospital Medical College in New York City where he completed his thesis and graduated in 1875. While the Whites wanted him to return promptly to Battle Creek and get the Institute back on a paying basis, the young doctor had other plans. He wanted to follow older brother Merritt's example and promote the cause by

Left: *Dr. John Harvey Kellogg, his wife Ella, and a canine friend posed for the camera in 1885. The couple compensated for their childless marriage by adopting and raising scores of orphans. Courtesy, Duff Stoltz*

Throughout the following six decades he published hundreds of papers and scores of books with a total sales of more than one million copies to become one of the country's most prolific medical authors. Kellogg achieved his prodigious output by seizing any spare moment to dash off a few paragraphs or to dictate a chapter. Pen and paper always lay by his bedside, a secretary accompanied him on his travels, and, reputedly, he even dictated from the water closet. His writings drew a popular following because, as one reviewer noted, Kellogg had "a happy way of popularizing the abstruse theories and technicalities of science in such lucid and felicitous language as to make his books entertaining as well as instructive."

Kellogg could muster the latest statistics and scientific evidence, coin descriptive new words, form persuasive analogies, and create sensational rhetoric to make his point, but throughout his long writing career few of his points changed. He continued to hammer away in support of the theories he learned while still a youth. He had been schooled in the best facilities available, traveled extensively, and stayed posted on new medical developments, but Sylvester Graham and Russell Trall had more impact on his professional attitudes than all of his advanced medical training. He maintained an implacable faith in the curative power of water, vegetables, and temperance. He coupled a morbid overemphasis on the digestive tract with an extremely conservative view of sexual functions. Kellogg's literary productions won a mass audience but never the full respect of his profession.

One of Kellogg's early books, *Dyspepsia, Its Causes, Prevention and Cure* (Battle Creek, 1879) suggests his preoccupation with the digestive system. "If the whole truth were shown," he wrote, "it would appear that the causes of indigestion are responsible for more deaths than all other causes combined." The average American, Kellogg told his readers, treated "his mouth like a corn-hopper and his stomach like a garbage-box." In 1887 his *Sunbeams of Health and Temperance* had a special message for female dyspeptics:

It isn't any wonder that your face is pale and haggard, your cheeks thin, your naturally fair skin covered all over with unsightly brown patches, and that you are so afflicted with general good-for-nothingness. Your blood is thin and poor for want of well-digested food. Your nerves are distracted with exciting and irritating condiments, and your liver is half paralyzed by its frantic efforts to dispose of some of the wretched stuff you have been putting into your stomach. The wonder is you have not died of starvation, of spinal anaemia, or inflammation of the stomach, or winter cholera, or some other proper kind of punishment for your unnatural treatment of your digestive organs.

Kellogg's *Sunbeams* devoted a good deal of space to the evils of condiments. Mustard, vinegar, pepper, ginger, curry, even salt were poisons. He garnered examples from around the world to illustrate their pernicious effects. The liberal use of curry powder by the British residents of India, Kellogg announced, gave rise to their morning salutation "How's your liver?" An American cavalryman presented a pickle to a half-starved Indian, who then tried to kill his benefactor. Even cold water, drunk at mealtimes, was bad. To Kellogg, diners downing glasses of water seemed to be trying to "drown out a ground squirrel that had surreptitiously taken possession of their inner man." Ice water, wrote Kellogg in 1891, "under certain circumstances acts with all the force and rapidity of prussic acid."

By the 1890s, as his book sales boomed, Kellogg detected a growing interest in everything relating to health, resulting, he sadly commented, "from the recognition of the fact that the race is positively deteriorating physically, if not mentally and morally." The moral element stood ever ready to shock Kellogg's readers. He frequently employed the concept of intoxication. Primitive tribesmen dined at "flesh banquets" and grew absolutely "intoxicated by meat." The British fondness to "spree on tea" resulted in many reported cases of tea drunkenness, even delerium tremens. In the 20th century Kellogg coined the word "autointoxication" to describe the intestinal effects of a rich diet.

Kellogg envisioned a constant relationship between diet and morality. The hearty Sunday dinners Americans enjoyed were "without doubt responsible for many forms of Sabbath breaking, as no individual can have a clear perception of right and a quick sense of wrong when laboring under the incubus of an over-loaded stomach." Children in their formative years were especially susceptible to derangement via diet. "The helpless infant imbibed the essence of libidinous desires with its mother's milk," and when weaned, the child's "tender organs of digestion were plied with highly seasoned viands, stimulating sauces, animal food, sweetmeats and dainty tidbits in endless variety." These exciting stimulants "reacted upon the sexual system with utmost certainty." "How many mothers," Kellogg lamented, "while teaching their children the principles of virtue in the nursery, unwittingly stimulate their passions at the dinner table until vice becomes almost a physical necessity."

Dr. Kellogg, however, reserved his finest moralizations and most vivid rhetoric for his best-selling sex manual, *Plain Facts About Sexual Life*. First published in 1877 as a 356-page volume, 25 years later it had run through 15 editions, sold 300,000 copies, and become a massive 800-page encyclopedia of morals. Few elements relating to the topic escaped Kellogg's scrutiny. Female flirtation he found "pernicious in the extreme," while male flirts were monsters, "loathsome social lepers who slowly wound their coils about their victims." "Filthy dreamers" who contemplated lascivious themes were "swept rapidly down the current of sensualism." Kellogg reached poetic heights when he dealt with the "filthy habit" of tobacco use: "when acquired early, it excites the undeveloped organs, arouses the passions, and in a few years converts the once chaste and pure youth into a veritable volcano of lust, belching out from its inner fires of passion, torrents of obscenity and the sulphurous fumes of lasciviousness."

The testimony in *Plain Facts* identifying innate characteristics as a source of vice is reminiscent of statements found throughout the *The Health Reformer*. "A drunkard begets in his child a thirst for liquor," Kellogg wrote, "and the child enters the world with a natural taste for intoxicants." "A thief transmits to his offspring a secretive, dishonest, sneaking disposition," and "the children of libertines are almost always certain to be rakes and prostitutes." As a result, Kellogg suggested that criminals ought to be barred from mating "by legislation or some other means." He later

amplified his views on uneugenic marriages by creating and funding a Race Betterment Foundation at the Sanitarium.

In addition to bad blood, flirting, and tobacco, Kellogg saw the nether regions of the alimentary canal as a potential source of vice. In constipation, he noted, lay "one of the most general physical causes of sexual excitement." He stressed throughout his writings that "the bowels should be emptied at least twice a day, and three or four movements are still better." Many of his books carried lively scatological discussions of prunes, enemas, and colon hygiene. Enemas of all descriptions had long been part of the hydropathic regimen, and Kellogg firmly believed in and relied on their efficacy. He saw the "house broke" colon as one of society's pressing problems. In 1918 Kellogg published a best-seller, *The Itinerary of a Breakfast*, in which he personally conducted an exploring party on "a trip with a slice of bread along the most wonderful subway in the world."

As he waged his campaign to change the intestinal flora of his countrymen, Kellogg found time to promote other theories that harkened back to his early indoctrination. Americans stood in danger of suffocation by being "squeezed to death by tight lacing" of corsets or in simple "chamber smothering." "During the cold season," he wrote in 1891, "the average bed chamber not infrequently becomes a veritable death trap." By 1912 his wife, Ella, when not actively pursuing her

The Calhoun County History, published in 1877, presented lithographs of the newly remodeled Battle Creek Sanitarium. To the right is the original Greek Revival farmhouse where the institution began in 1866. The large Italianate additions were among Dr. Kellogg's innovations. Courtesy, Larry B. Massie

duties as Superintendent of Mother's Work of the National WCTU, assisted Kellogg in his fight for "fresh air sleeping." Her articles in *Good Health* advocated a sleeping arrangement with the head thrust out an open bedroom window. Alternative arrangements included window tents and "fresh air tubes," which carried outside air to shivering sleepers.

In 1913 Dr. Kellogg turned to the subject of cancer in his monograph, *The Monster Malady....* He identified this "coming plague of the race" as confined to civilized men and domesticated animals. Humans got cancer because they ate animal flesh. In vegetarianism, the simple life, and hydropathy resided the cure.

Next to diet reform, hydrotherapy remained Kellogg's most recommended panacea. Most of

One of the high spots of a stay at the Battle Creek Sanitarium was Dr. Kellogg's evening "Health Question Box" during which he extemporaneously responded to the audience's health concerns. Here the camera records a 1924 performance by the flamboyant doctor. Courtesy, Michigan Room, Willard Public Library

Kellogg's 20th-century statements concerning the curative powers of the water treatment could have come straight from the pens of Joel Shew, Russell Trall, or James Jackson. Kellogg's older brother, Merritt, wrote a book on hydropathy in 1873 in which he described more than 40 baths suitable for medical treatments including: the sitz bath, dripping-sheet bath, cataract douche, plunge bath, wet girdle, fomentations, and electrical bath. Hot and cold vertical rain douches, now known as showers, were popular remedies for decades. The horizontal rain douche required an assistant who leveled a stream of water from a high-pressure hose at afflicted portions of the anatomy.

Another longtime hydropathic favorite was the salt glow. W.B. Hill, a run-down Adventist preacher from Minnesota who arrived at the Sanitarium in 1884, recalled a typical treatment.

After a warm bath and a cold bath during which he thought his "breath would forsake him, never more to return," he got the salt glow. "I stood on a stool and took hold, with my hands of iron hooks in the wall above my head, while my attendant took handfuls of salt, mixed with water until it was like mush, and rubbed me with it from head to foot until there was a redness all over me. It was quite a severe process, as the sharp salt crystals would almost cut through the skin." Next came a warm shower, a cold shower, and a massage. He "enjoyed" the electric bath most of all. As he lay full length in tepid water, the attendant applied electrical charges to his chest and then extremities. Hill felt as if he was "being rejuvenated."

Other patients sought rejuvenation through steam baths. Elder Hill remembered the day when the Sanitarium "resounded with whoops and yells and very unbecoming words, and short sentences delivered with all the energy of a Boanerges." The attendants had turned on the steam and forgotten about a visiting Confederate general from Georgia. In 1893 Ruby Mathews wrote a friend back in Fenton, Michigan, "they put me in a steam box last Thursday and steamed me—I just had my head out—well I thought they were going to kill me sure—and you can tell that it was severe for I could not stand alone for quite a while and was weak all day."

Exercise comprised another element of the Battle Creek curriculum. By the turn of the century trainers imported from the old country supervised a Swedish movement cure that offered calisthenics for the treatment of disease. A typical daily ritual at the Sanitarium began with chest gymnastics at 7:00 a.m., and throughout the day patients reported back to the gymnasium for scheduled drills, marches, games, and laughing exercises. The evening concluded with the "Grand March" to the tune of Samuel Siegel's *Battle Creek Sanitarium March*. Young Edson Knight spied on his parents in the gymnasium one morning in 1898. "You ought to see the movements they have to go through with," he wrote a friend back home. "The gym teacher had them walk as fast as they could and not run. One old woman came very near falling down." Long before aerobic dancing became a fad, Kellogg developed a system of

Left: *Battle Creek residents strolling past the Sanitarium were frequently startled by scenes such as this, as patients turned out en masse for exercise. Courtesy, Michigan Room, Willard Public Library*

"exercising to music." In the 1920s he marketed "The Health Ladder," a series of phonograph records containing music and directions for 20 exercises.

Hours of exercise, steam baths, and electrical treatments gave Sanitarium guests a ravenous appetite. Perhaps only those with such an appetite could have enjoyed the meals. By the 1890s Kellogg had dressed up the bill of fare, but the Grahamite origins were still obvious. Breakfast entrées included stewed prunes, hot gluten mush, avenola, wheatena, oatmeal crackers, dyspeptic wafers, and graham rolls, bread, crackers, gems or grits all washed down with caramel coffee or lemon oatmeal gruel. A few years later Kellogg introduced a beverage made from a species of South African grass, Kaffir tea. "It looks like tea," traveling journalist Julian Street wrote in 1914, "and would probably taste like it too, if they didn't let the Kaffirs steep so long. But they should use only fresh, young, tender Kaffirs; the old ones get too strong; they have too much bouquet. The one they used in my tea may have been slightly spoiled. I tasted him all afternoon." "The joy of eating at Battle Creek," Kellogg's advertisements boasted, lay in the fact that "every meal is a prescription."

"Flesh foods" were not tolerated at Sanitarium tables because they carried "into the colon countless numbers of pernicious putrefactive bacteria." But Kellogg worked long and hard to develop a meat substitute that "would

deceive the connoisseur." He came up with savita, a flavoring for soups, protose, which "looks, tastes, and smells like meat," and nuttolene, made from ground nuts. Julian Street's helping of nuttolene resembled "a good sized piece of shoe-maker's wax. In flavor it is confusing. Some faint taste about it hinted it was intended to resemble turkey; an impression furthered by the fact that cranberry sauce was served on the same plate. But what it was made of I could not detect. It was not unpleasant to taste, nor yet did I find it appetizing. Rather, I should classify it in the broad category of uninteresting food."

Above: *At the turn of the century, the "Swedish Movement" room of the Battle Creek Sanitarium featured diverse and fiendish exercise machines that stretched and pulled patients back to health. Dr. Kellogg's bucking horse invention was favored for exercise by President Coolidge. Courtesy, Michigan Room, Willard Public Library*

Dr. Kellogg, dressed in spotless white, stands while distinguished guests prepare to enjoy a health food banquet at his Sanitarium, around 1910. The menu offered no meat, tea, coffee, or spirits. Courtesy, Michigan Room, Willard Public Library

On Thanksgiving Day, 1901, more than 1,100 Sanitarium guests sat down to Fletcherize a "feast without slaughter" in celebration of the 35th anniversary of the institution. The menu featured nut roast, nuttolene fricassee, sliced protose, and plenty of graham bread and concluded with mixed nuts. While the guests munched their fare, a live turkey gobbled a similar meal from his place of honor at the speaker's platform. "The first and true idea of Thanksgiving," announced the guest speaker, Professor Percy T. Magan, "is not to eat turkey, which is corn second-hand, but to eat the corn itself, first hand." As the audience cheered, the turkey "flapped his wings lustily."

Kellogg's popular journal, *Good Health*, carried advertisements by the page for his strange-sounding foods. In 1912, nestled among advertisements for "magic pocket vaporizers," "hygienic phondates," a sterile mouthpiece that warded off diseases passed through promiscuous use of the phone, and Sharp and Smith's "Anti-snoring apparatus," a bandage that clamped the snorer's mouth shut, were columns of health food concoctions. The obese could order bags of gluten flour and the run-down his vitamin breakfast cereal, Zo. For the irregular, a Kellogg specialy, he offered Fig Bran Flakes, bran-agar biscuits called Laxa, and Para-Lax, a mineral oil. Kellogg's quest for better-tasting health foods eventually compromised his long-held views concerning the evils of iced foods and condiments. By 1920, amidst jellied prunes, cream of gluten mush, and potato gruel, the Sanitarium menu proffered broiled protose with chili sauce and fruit ice.

Weight-watchers found Sanitarium menus much to their liking. In 1904, shortly after calorie measuring techniques had been perfected, Kellogg began listing the protein, fat, and carbohydrate makeup of each entrée. That year Ella Kellogg produced *Healthful Cookery*, which contained recipes utilizing her husband's array of meat substitutes. In 1914 Lenna Frances Cooper, head dietitian at the Sanitarium, published one of the first cookbooks to measure the calories in each item. *The New Cookery*, which went through 11 editions by 1929, included recipes for hundreds of the vegetarian dishes served at the Sanitarium. These Sanitarium-oriented cookbooks had been preceded by Almeda Lambert's *Guide for Nut Cookery* (Battle Creek, 1899). Mrs. Lambert taught homemakers how to transform nuts into main dishes, including mock salmon molded to resemble a whole fish on the platter. Almeda's husband, Joseph, had left the buggy-making business to capitalize on one of Kellogg's patented inventions, peanut butter. In 1895 he began marketing nut-grinding machines and peanuts. By the turn of the century he conducted a prosperous nut food business from his newly erected block at 235 West Main Street. Lambert manufactured nut-butter mills, blanching machines, and peanut roasters as well as nut butter, malted caramels, and crystal nuts.

As Kellogg relinquished the nut-butter industry to the Lamberts, his health empire attracted other competitors. In 1899 a small army of masons began constructing a huge fieldstone structure just down the street from the Sanitarium. Neil S. Phelps, president of the Ellis Publishing Company, had decided to run the Sanitarium out of business. His brother, Dr. O.S. Phelps, left his post at a private sanatorium in New York City to head the medical staff, and in 1900 the Phelps Medical and Surgical Sanatorium opened its doors. Phelps offered alternatives to Kellogg's ascetic fare. Roast beef and cups of strong coffee supplanted nuttolene and Kaffir tea, and smoking rooms vied with anti-tobaccoism. Within four years the Phelps Sanatorium went broke.

In 1908 the fieldstone hospital reopened, this time under the flamboyant direction of America's prototype strongman, Bernarr Macfadden. The ex-wrestler who spent a lifetime extolling the virtues of good posture and deep breathing while posing bare chested, had decided to muscle in on the Battle Creek market. He came up with "Strengtho," a hot breakfast cereal, and

Above: A booth in John Harvey Kellogg's "San" during the 1920s made available for home consumption the variety of strange-sounding health foods he had invented, as well as copies of his more than 50 medical guides. Courtesy, Michigan Room, Willard Public Library

Left: In 1926 John Harvey Kellogg's Good Health magazine carried an advertisement for the health foods he invented. Most of the foods were made from some form of nut and catered to those with colon problems. Courtesy, Larry B. Massie

the Macfadden Health Home. Strengtho, which turned rancid on the shelf, lasted about as long as the Health Home. Soon the fieldstone hospital became the Battle Creek Sanitarium Annex. In 1921 Macfadden's second Battle Creek venture, a health institute located at the edge of Camp Custer, proved no more successful. Ironically, the king of physical culture later acquired Jackson's Home on the Hillside in Dansville, New York, which had been the model for Kellogg's Sanitarium.

Unrelated namesake Frank J. Kellogg offered particularly embarrassing competition for Dr. Kellogg. Known locally as Anti-Fat Kellogg, although he also marketed an anti-lean nostrum, Frank Kellogg operated a quack mail-

PROTOSE
—— A ——
VEGETABLE
MEAT

A pure, wholesome food, made from nuts

and cereals, possessing all the nutritive value of the choicest steak and lacking in none of its delicious flavors would be ideal, wouldn't it?

That's Protose. Just like meat only better. You miss nothing but the bone and gristle.

Can be boiled, broiled and stewed or prepared in many other delightful ways.

A sample will be sent to any one on request.

THE KELLOGG FOOD COMPANY.,

Dept. 0-2

Battle Creek, Michigan

Dr. Kellogg experimented for decades to develop a vegetarian meat substitute. Diners at his Battle Creek Sanitarium discovered the joys of protose, nuttolene, and savita, all made from nuts. Courtesy, Larry B. Massie

order scheme. Full-column advertisements in newspapers and magazines boldly lettered "Don't Stay Fat" depicted the traditional before-and-after profiles. Following the passage of the Pure Food and Drug Act of 1906, Kellogg dropped the title of professor from his name. "Kellogg's Obesity Food" became "Kellogg Safe Fat Reducer" when Washington chemists found it to be not a "food" but a mixture of toasted bread crumbs, thyroid gland, and poke root. Kellogg also offered Sanitone Wafers, "the greatest nerve vitalizer known," and Multo-Fruto, "Nature's delicious laxative." When consumers responded to the free trial package offer, they received a small sample and in the same mail an unsolicited "complete thirty day treatment" with a five-dollar billing. Kellogg then dunned them for months with threatening letters. The sale of bogus cures reputedly made Anti-Fat Kellogg a millionaire.

The period's grandest medical scams began when James M. Peebles, "the spiritual pilgrim," returned to the scene of his earlier glories. Peebles had gathered no moss since he relinquished his ministerial duties at Battle Creek's spiritualist church in 1867. The following year he collaborated with J.O. Barrett to publish in Boston a spiritualist hymn book, *The Spiritual Harp.* For some reason President Grant appointed him United States Consul to Trebinzonde, a Turkish Black Sea port, in 1869. Peebles retained his charge briefly, "until he became sick of Turkish indolence and filth." He stayed on the move, journeying at least three times around the world to observe "the laws, customs, and religions of nations and people, giving special attention to spiritualism, magic, and theosophy." During his second world voyage Peebles "studied the occult forces and chronic diseases in China and Siam; the prevailing fevers of India and Ceylon; leprosy in Madras, Bangalore, Kilpank and the hospitals of Oriental countries." These experiences combined with many years of spiritualist communication with noted deceased physicians of all ages "lessened his drugs and increased his faith in the psychic treatment."

"The soul and soul forces," Peebles decided, were the "great healers." He paused from his travels to pick up a quick diploma from the fraudulent Philadelphia University of Medicine and Surgery in 1876. Dr. Peebles then bounced around the country, setting up psychic healing institutes at Hammonton, New Jersey; San Antonio, Texas; and San Diego, California. In 1896 the 73-year-old white-bearded giant, resembling "King Lear tailored by Brooks Brothers," landed back in Battle Creek. He wasted no time in setting up Dr. Peebles Institute at 350 Madison Street with the motto "Health is the foundation of success"—his own continued success, Peebles hoped.

Lavishly illustrated promotional pamphlets informed sufferers that the institute gave special attention to "afflictions peculiar to either sex, to kidneys, liver, stomach, catarrh, asthma, blood, skin, and nervous diseases." Peebles took Dr. J.A. Burroughs and his wife, Bertha, as partners. Burroughs, Peebles' adopted son and a "pupil and companion in his travels," possessed occult powers of "determining the secret cause of chronic disease." Ladies who preferred "the counsel of their own sex in certain matters" might enlist the similar skills of Mrs. Dr. Burroughs, who looked like a carnival queen but whose "marked gifts have never been paraded before the public." Dr. Peebles himself tackled "cases of peculiar nature in which no ordinary method of relief is efficient."

"The brain is the seat of life," Peebles assured prospective clients, "the storage battery that supplies every nerve and fiber of the system with nervo-vitality." The Peebles-Burroughs approach allied medical science with mediumship to focus psychic powers "with determination until the all important question is settled." Once their diseases were settled, patients paid "modest sums as can not embarrass"—others, seeking health on the installment plan, could "pay as they go." Individuals unable to visit the institute merely sent in a description of their complaints with prepayment, and the mediums sent back a diagnosis and cure. "Hundreds of patients who have been speedily cured," Peebles noted, "have never seen the doctors who treated them."

A few years later, when Peebles claimed he had the power of Christ to cure all ills and even restore life, he went too far. In 1901 a grand jury indicted "the spiritual pilgrim" and hauled him into the United States District Court in Detroit. In 1949 veteran Detroit journalist Malcolm Bingay, who covered the trial as his first assignment, recalled the sensational court proceedings:

District Attorney Gordon bellowed at Peebles on the stand: "Do you, before this jury of God-fearing men, now claim, under oath, that you have the powers of our Lord and Savior Jesus Christ, to heal the sick and restore the dead to Life?"

Peebles rose from the chair to his full height of six feet four and raised his fist above his head. He looked like Moses in a Cecil de Mille super-colossal. "I do!" he cried in a rich baritone voice that reverberated through the old court chambers. "I do! And may God strike me dead on this spot if I am not possessed of such power! He gave it to me. Speak, O God, and give this jury the proof! The proof!"

The jury and I waited for divine action. The air was tense. . . . Peebles stood there with his arm still high, waiting, waiting, waiting. For about a minute he stood, then relaxed. He turned to the jury in a soft purring voice and said: "Gentlemen, you see for yourself."

Despite his courtroom showmanship the jury convicted Peebles of practicing fraudulent medicine. It hardly slowed his career. He shifted from mail-order diagnosis to a carefully worded mail-order patent medicine racket—the Peebles Epilepsy Cure. Peebles took a new partner, W.T. Bobo, M.D., who made his living marketing a mail-order goiter cure. Advertisements headlined "Fits" featured Peebles' bewhiskered countenance on the double-barreled cure. Preparation "No. 1" was a "brain restorative" and "No. 2" a "nerve tonic." "Let the remedies speak for themselves" urged the advertisements, but when Pure Food and Drug Act chemists analyzed the mixtures they found "No. 1" largely an alcoholic tincture flavored with bitter almonds and "No. 2" a sweetened watery solution of vegetable products with no active characteristics. They declared the remedies misbranded and fined the company. By 1915 Peebles had wandered out to Los Angeles to pursue his profession. In 1922 the colorful author of *How to Live a Century and Grow Old Gracefully* died one month short of his 100th birthday.

The years during which Peebles plied his Battle Creek shenanigans had also been busy ones for Dr. Kellogg. Following a fire that leveled the main Sanitarium building in 1902, he erected a six-story fireproof structure able to accommodate more than 1,000 guests. A breach with the church over control of the Sanitarium resulted in Kellogg's excommunication in 1907. Undaunted, he continued to expand, acquiring the Phelps-Macfadden fieldstone hospital as an annex in 1911, and in 1915, the year Ellen White died, Kellogg opened a new 75-bed hospital building. Kellogg's appearance evolved as well. He eschewed his rather shaggy beard of

John Harvey Kellogg's popular medical journal, Good Health, *carried page after page of advertisements for exotic devices such as this 1911 Sharp and Smith specimen. Courtesy, Larry B. Massie*

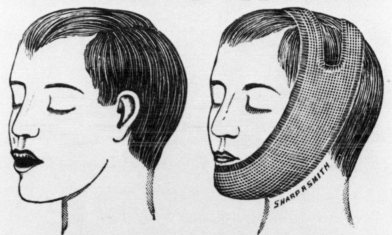

Right: *Eleanor Roosevelt observes the scientific preparation of food at the Battle Creek Sanitarium kitchen, circa 1935. Mrs. Roosevelt was one of scores of famous visitors to the world-famous health mecca. Courtesy, Duff Stoltz*

Above: *Each evening patients at the Battle Creek Sanitarium enjoyed the highlight of their health-restoring regimen: "the hop at the top," which featured group dancing on the Sanitarium roof. Courtesy, Michigan Room, Willard Public Library*

the 19th century for a closely trimmed Van Dyk goatee. As time bleached his whiskers, the diminutive doctor followed sartorially by dressing in white from head to foot.

The Roaring Twenties brought the glory days of Battle Creek's health mecca. In 1920 the Sanitarium could report having serviced 143,643 patients over the previous 44 years. By the end of the decade a Sanitarium staff of 1,800 catered to nearly 15,000 clients who checked in for their annual "health inventory." Ex-presidents, governors, congressmen, industrial magnates, famous athletes, and entertainers arrived for a "Battle Creek vacation" to "eat,

sleep and live daily for health."

Kellogg's most expansive undertaking came in 1928 when the Sanitarium's new 15-story "Central Building" dominated the Battle Creek skyline. It was a monument to "biologic living" in Italian Renaissance and Florentine architecture. From a classical colonade extending its entire length to the rooftop "pergola promenade" where the evening's cool breezes fanned grand marchers, the structure groaned with luxurious trimmings. The two-story-high main lobby featured a dozen Mankato marble pillars, crystal chandeliers, chintz draperies, hand-painted classical friezes, two enormous marble wall clocks, and plush Oriental rugs. Guests awaiting a vegetarian meal or a turn in the steam cabinet reclined on overstuffed chairs amidst potted palms. The 268 guest rooms boasted running ice water, alcoves for fresh-air sleeping, and special "vita glass" windows which admitted healing ultra-violet rays of sunlight. Mr. Henry Ford of Detroit and his wife, Clara, became the first guests to check in, followed by Commander Richard E. Byrd of Antarctic fame, and Eddie Cantor.

The plush central building carried a price tag of $3 million in bonded indebtedness. The Sanitarium's plunge from its frugal origins into the glittering jazz age might have been successful were the timing better. But when 1929 brought the stock market crash and a decade of depression, well-heeled guests became very scarce. Kellogg struggled to stay solvent, laid off staff members, and paid those who stayed on in scrip. But on January 1, 1933, the Sanitarium defaulted on its bonded obligations. It was placed under receivership and reorganized the following year as the Battle Creek Sanitarium and Benevolent Association. Somehow Kellogg kept the institution operating through the remainder of the Depression.

By the 1940s, as the Sanitarium population shrank to 300 patients, the time had come for retrenchment. The U.S. Army purchased the main Sanitarium structure as a base hospital, which opened on May 15, 1942, as Percy Jones General Hospital. Kellogg's remaining employees assisted by city firemen carted the furnishings and equipment down the street to the fieldstone annex, and a smaller but financially stable Sanitarium was back in the business of health.

The following year a bitter court battle erupted when the Adventist Church sought to gain control of the Sanitarium and its tempting one-million-dollar treasury. The 91-year-old Kellogg marshaled all his assets to wage what became the last campaign to keep his Sanitarium. He won the battle but, weakened by the effort, died on December 14, 1943. Ironically, W.K. Kellogg, who had launched his own spectacular career on one of his older brother's health food creations, also died at the age of 91 in 1951. But the life of W.K. Kellogg and the rise of the mighty Battle Creek cereal industry is another story.

Left: *An 1898 edition of John Harvey Kellogg's* Ladies' Guide in Health and Disease *carried a frontispiece portrait of the dynamic little doctor. Within a few years his hirsute countenance would be modified with a Vandyke goatee. Courtesy, Larry B. Massie*

Below: *Battle Creek still cherished its image as a health center in 1930 as this view of the Post Tavern taken from the Good Health Cafeteria testified. The ruins to the right were leveled in preparation for construction of the Central Bank Tower, now Transamerica Tower, in 1932. Courtesy, Michigan Room, Willard Public Library*

CHAPTER V

The Cereal City

THE bugle call that brings all the little troopers eagerly around the mess-table is Kellogg's Toasted Corn Flakes.

Kellogg's — the Original Toasted Corn Flakes, remain as original as ever — light, and dainty, appetizing in flavor, with a melting crispness on the tongue.

Imitations come and go! They change their name They change their form Some do both Why?

W. K. Kellogg

Kellogg's TOASTED CORN FLAKES

here is a taste of Heaven in perfect health and a taste of Hell in sickness," wrote Charles William Post, and in 1891, as his wife pushed his wheelchair about the streets of Battle Creek, he was tasting Hell. Post had been laid low by a bout of chronic dyspepsia. But it was not the first time illness had interrupted the career of the 37-year-old invalid.

Post grew up in Springfield, Illinois, where he attended the local schools and the predecessor of the University of Illinois for a spell. He joined the Springfield Zouaves, a state militia unit, and served with them on active duty during the Chicago fire. In 1874 he married Ella Letitia Merriweather, who later bore their only child, Marjorie. Post embarked on a career typical of a 19th-century entrepreneur with wanderlust. As he bounded around the country seeking his fortune, he invented variations on the plow blade, bicycle, and player piano and a type of "invisible" suspenders. He went bankrupt manufacturing "Post Capital City Cultivators" at Springfield and left for Texas with his brother, Carroll, for a new start. At Fort Worth they sold lots in their newly platted subdivision and bought into a woolen blanket mill. But in the 1880s, just when it appeared one of his ventures might prove successful, he suffered a physical breakdown— nervous prostration or dyspepsia. He had tried cures ranging from mineral water spas to Swedish movements, and desperation drew him to Battle Creek's nationally touted health mecca.

Post's funds were about as low as his health. To save money the family checked into a near-by rooming house, and Post swapped a supply of blankets left over from his Texas venture for a dose of the Sanitarium regimen. Meanwhile Ella hawked his invisible galluses door to door. Post sampled Kellogg's hydrotherapy, health foods, and lectures on right eating and thinking. He found the lectures stimulating and the meals bland. But two items on the bill of fare sparked his interest—Granola and Caramel Cereal Coffee (both of which, incidentally, descended along with the idea for the Sanitarium from Dr. Jackson's Dansville, New York, Home on the Hillside). In the early 1860s Jackson's patients had enjoyed "Granula," twice-baked graham bread crumbs, and "Somo," a cereal-based coffee substitute.

When nine months of Sanitarium life brought little change in Post's health, he tried some of Battle Creek's other medicinal practitioners, including a Christian Scientist and a pair of clairvoyants. Evidently the power of positive thinking worked where enemas had failed. Post decided that no matter how ill he looked, "the only way to get well was to be well," and he "began walking around like a man who had business to attend to." That business included a proposal to team up with Dr. Kellogg to promote his cereal coffee. When Kellogg flatly refused the offer, Post proceeded to go into the health business himself.

In May 1892 he acquired the Grenville Beardsley estate, a 10-acre homestead on the east side of the city. The Italianate farmhouse became "La Vita Inn," a medical boardinghouse where Post plied his newly learned curative powers. Post practiced a mix of Kelloggism, Christian Science, positive thought, and a form of biofeedback utilizing "mental negation," "the energy of your divine selfhood," and a dash of electricity. He succeeded in galvanizing a number of sufferers from rheumatism, dyspepsia, ulcerated teeth, and bladder complaints back onto "the road to Wellville." By 1893 Post had codified his medical philosophy into a hardcover volume imprinted at La Vita Inn, *I Am Well*. Human emotions consisted of negative and positive currents, Post explained. "The negative currents are thoughts of anger, hate, grief, anxiety, jealousy, apprehension, sensuality, disease, etc. These negative currents are disease producing and tend to destroy and throw out through the pores and other excretory channels the valuable parts or elements in the nerve centers, and deplete and exhaust the battery, so to speak." While staring fixedly into their eyes Post told his patients, "There is a power within you that can and will work miracles." He also dosed them with hot helpings of a beverage very similar to the Sanitarium's Caramel Cereal Coffee.

The guests at La Vita Inn evidently liked the blend so well that Post determined to stake his future on the beverage. In December 1894 he bought a secondhand gasoline stove for roasting bran, a small hand-operated peanut roaster for roasting wheat, an old-fashioned coffee grinder, and several mixers—total capital

investment, $46.85. He also spent $21.91 on two bushels of wheat, 200 pounds of bran, 10 jugs of molasses, 50 packing cases, and 200 cartons. Post installed his machinery in a little Greek-revival horse barn adjacent to the inn, roasted up a batch, and began peddling paper bags of his product on the streets of Battle Creek from a pushcart.

While other proprietors might choose high-sounding appellations like Somo, Panamalt, or Minute Brew for their coffee substitutes, Post simply named his Postum. The half-century-long war Dr. Kellogg and the vegetable reformers had waged against coffee gained a brilliant propagandist in Post. "Any analytical chemist can show that coffee and tea contain a poisonous drug—caffeine," early Postum advertising warned, "which belongs in the same class of alkaloids with cocaine, morphine, nicotine and strychnine." "It is safe to say," said Post, who wrote all his own advertising copy, "that one person in every three among coffee users has some incipient or advanced form of disease."

By February 1895 Post was in Grand Rapids demonstrating Postum. He spent 20 minutes boiling a pot in the office of W.H. Turner, editor of the Grand Rapids *Evening News,* and left with $1,000 in advertising credit. When "Furniture City" grocery jobber E.J. Herrick balked at his product, Post turned his refusal into a new advertising slogan. Herrick advised him, "Save your money, young man, have fun with it, or go into some business that there is some reason for. You simply cannot make anybody ask for an instead-of-coffee cereal drink." Post launched a vigorous advertising campaign under the mysterious motto, "There's a reason," but never explained that reason to the public. Later, in the office of a Chicago editor, Post faced a similar lack of confidence. But when the dubious editor noticed a small red dot and the statement "It makes red blood" on the upper right corner of the Postum letterhead, he caught the fever and granted Post $10,000 in advertising credit. As Post coined new names for old diseases, readers with palpitations, headaches, or lack of energy learned they had "coffee heart," "coffee neuralgia," and "brain fag." The "grandfather of modern advertising" bombarded the media with clever pitches and sunk most of his early profits back into more

Facing page: *J.C. Leyendecker, who illustrated over 400* Saturday Evening Post *covers beginning in 1915, created a patriotic youth for Kellogg Company's advertising in 1917 as the U.S. geared up for World War I. Leyendecker drew 16 more children for Kellogg Company's advertisements during the World War I years. Copyright, 1984, courtesy, Kellogg Company*

copy.

At the end of the first year of production, total sales for Postum stood at $5,000. The following year they reached $265,000. In 1898 consumers bought $840,000 worth. That year Post introduced his second cereal product—Grape Nuts—née Granula, née Granola. Curiously, he first tried advertising Grape Nuts as a cereal beverage, which, "when properly brewed, takes the beautiful deep seal-brown color of Mocha or Java, changing to a rich golden brown when cream is added." But the product won greater acceptance when he shifted to promoting Grape Nuts as a cold breakfast food. Early packages of Grape Nuts contained a miniature pamphlet, "The Road to Wellville," a synopsis of *I Am Well.* In 1900 Car-

When C.W. Post introduced Post Toasties in 1908 he hired teams of delivery boys to carry free packages of the cereal door-to-door. Courtesy, Michigan Room, Willard Public Library

roll Post joined his brother as sales manager. By 1901 Post was spending $400,000 on advertising and clearing nearly one million dollars a year.

To keep pace with the galloping growth in sales Post went into a hectic building program. The first warehouse constructed in 1898 was followed by acres of production plants, grain storage buildings, endless conveyor belts, and railroad sidings. To supply the tons of packages and cartons, in 1899 Post started his own paper mill, the Battle Creek Paper Company, later the carton and container division of Post Products. The following year Post installed his own power plant consisting of four boilers and three steam engines driving generators. Soon nearby windows rattled and teams ran away as a high-pitched steam whistle called hundreds of

Postum employees to work. Post offered area farmers five cents a bushel more than the going rate to guarantee a steady supply of fine quality wheat, and long lines of farm wagons delivering grain to the factory became a familiar sight. An enclosed overhead wheat conveyor that ran from the grain tower to the bakery appeared in 1902. Post dubbed it "the road to Wellville."

Following a policy of self-sufficiency, Post created his own advertising unit in 1903, and the following year the Grandin Advertising Agency occupied a newly constructed English half-timbered Club House. The sprawling Postum Cereal Company, its buildings painted dazzling white with green trim reminiscent of the Columbian Exposition, became known as the "white city." Claims that Postum products were "never touched by human hands in the process of manufacturing" drew crowds of welcome visitors to the carefully maintained plant. Sightseers sniffed the air fragrant with toasting bran, filed by the huge rumbling production lines, and followed paths that wound through the manicured landscape to the Club House to view Post's museum-quality collection of antique furniture, marble busts, and valuable paintings. Back home they boiled Postum and crunched Grape Nuts while recounting the exciting Battle Creek sights.

Post's third cereal product, introduced in 1906, met with far less success. He borrowed another of Kellogg's health food inventions, cornflakes, which he made a little thicker and blistered to stay crisper in milk. Post chose a name with a biblical flavor, Elijah's Manna, and packaged his cornflakes in green and white containers depicting a flock of ravens carrying the food from heaven to a bearded prophet. Post, who had grown up in the Midwest, should have known better. Ministers thundered from the pulpit against sacrilegious advertising, and the British government found Post in contempt of a law prohibiting the use of biblical names for commercial purposes. Post remedied his miscalculation in 1908, when Elijah's Manna became Post Toasties. Packages containing the same product portrayed an inoffensive young miss and her cat enjoying a bowl of cornflakes while seated before the hearth. Orders poured in from the Bible Belt and everywhere else for Post's "new" cereal. Nineteen-twelve saw the introduction of Instant Postum, another hit, and Post Tavern Porridge, a flop.

Post Tavern Porridge drew its name from a more successful venture launched in 1901. As a traveling man, Post remembered many a dull night spent in dreary hotels. He decided downtown Battle Creek would have one of the best hotels money could build. As local sidewalk superintendents scoffed at "Post's folly," a six-story, brick-and-stone hotel sprang up on the southwest corner of West Michigan Avenue and McCamly Street. In addition to 35 rooms and 40 private baths, the deluxe Post Tavern featured an English-style pub, an elegant ladies' parlor carpeted in delft blue, a Lincoln room with a display of Civil War artifacts, and a huge bridge room where 130 couples could dance or play cards after a banquet.

More than a luxurious hostelry, the Post Tavern competed with the Sanitarium as a retreat for the jaded. "Come and spend a summer at the Post Tavern," urged early promotional literature, where "tired and worn-out men and women can come and rest and be fed back to strength and comfort by expert food makers, who know how to select the right kind of food to rebuild worn out nerve centers." In opposition to Sanitarium fare, Post Tavern chefs gave "small favor to the bran, charcoal wafer, and cold porridge form of fanaticism in diet." By 1909 guests could breakfast on broiled kippered herring, salt mackerel, sugar-cured ham, calves' liver and bacon, calves' brains and scrambled eggs, or Grape Nuts griddle cakes. Commensurate with the plush surroundings, rates at the Post Tavern ran from $2.50 to $4 a night at a time when factory workers earned approximately $2 for a 10-hour day.

The Post Tavern proved so popular that a 10-story annex was added in 1911. A tile-roofed enclosed bridge stretched across McCamly Street to link the hotel with Post's office building. For decades the Post Tavern remained one of the finest hotels in the Midwest. But when automobiles supplanted trains, the convenience of outlying motels brought the demise of most downtown hotels. In 1960 the original six-story structure was razed, and the annex followed a decade later, yet old-time traveling men still speak of the glories of a stay at the Post Tavern.

In 1902 Post partially financed and lent his name to another downtown structure. Located

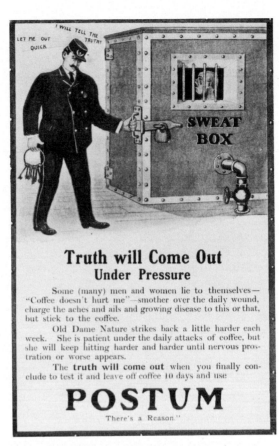

Truth will Come Out
Under Pressure

Some (many) men and women lie to themselves—"Coffee doesn't hurt me"—smother over the daily wound, charge the aches and ails and growing disease to this or that, but stick to the coffee.

Old Dame Nature strikes back a little harder each week. She is patient under the daily attacks of coffee, but she will keep hitting harder and harder until nervous prostration or worse appears.

The **truth will come out** when you finally conclude to test it and leave off coffee 10 days and use

POSTUM

"There's a Reason."

The June 1905 issue of Everybody's Magazine *carried a full-page Postum advertisement typical of C.W. Post's campaign against the evils of coffee drinking. Courtesy, Larry B. Massie*

adjacent to the Post Tavern, the Post Theatre became the finest legitimate playhouse between Detroit and Chicago. The same year the gala opening performance of the Post Theatre played to a full house, Post launched a real-estate venture that again placed his name on the Battle Creek map—the Post Addition. The cereal magnate acquired an 80-acre tract south of his plant and platted a subdivision. Lots sold for $150 to $450.

The Post Addition was not so much a money-making scheme as an attempt to foster good employee relations. Post intended to build a town for his workers. He constructed substantial two-story dwellings in the fashionable Queen Anne and Colonial Revival styles and offered them to employees at cost. Postum workers could purchase a six-to-eight-room home at prices ranging from $800 to $3,000. Buyers set up a payment schedule to suit their income, and when the last payment was made they received the deed. Down payments ran as low as $5 and monthly payments from $8 to $30. Other Battle Creek residents could purchase lots at slightly higher prices. The self-

made millionaire articulated his philosophy of giving, "The welfare work I believe in is that which makes it possible for the man to help himself." Post later fostered pride among homeowners by offering cash prizes for those who best maintained their homes, lawns, and gardens. By 1915 more than 81 percent of Postum employees owned their homes.

Post planned a real-estate development on a more massive scale in 1906. He returned to the scene of his earlier bankruptcy to purchase more than 200,000 acres of ranch land located 250 miles north of Fort Worth, Texas. The nearest railroad lay 70 miles away, but a model town, Post City, grew out of construction material carted in by mule train. Post built a two-story hotel and a cotton mill, and offered farmhouses and fencing at a low down payment. His Double U Company, headquartered in Battle Creek, chartered special railway excursions to Texas for prospective settlers to get a look at the site. The trip was free if they bought property. Half a century after its founding, Post City comprised a pleasant tree-shaded community of 4,800 residents surrounded by cotton fields and oil derricks.

In 1902 Post semi-retired from the management of the Postum Cereal Company to leave the reins in the hands of an able "cabinet" he had selected. This left him free to pursue his real-estate ventures, experiment with rain making by blowing off dynamite blasts, and travel. He maintained a suite at the Post Tavern, a

summer home in Greenwich, Connecticut, a winter estate in Santa Barbara, California, and offices in New York, Washington, and London. By 1914, as trains carrying 200 million packages of Postum products a year pulled out of Battle Creek, Post's assets stood at $70 million. But all his wealth could not buy good health. Periodically his lifelong struggle with stomach trouble flared up. Following a severe attack, an emergency cross-country train trip to the Mayo Clinic, and a prognosis of several months of pain, Post ended his own life at his Santa Barbara home on May 9, 1914.

His only child, Marjorie Merriweather Post, inherited her father's fortune. Her life became an American saga fully as colorful as C.W. Post's meteoric rise. She married and divorced four times while pursuing a course of unbridled luxury. While in Russia with her third husband, Joseph E. Davies, ambassador to the Soviet Union during the 1930s, she acquired a world-famous collection of Faberge, porcelain, glassware, and other Russian art treasures. She dotted America with luxurious mansions, traveled the world in a 350-foot-long sailing yacht, *The Sea Cloud,* and became renowned for her free-wheeling, big-spending, life-style. During the 1920s with the assistance of her second husband, E.F. Hutton, she parlayed the Postum Cereal Company into the nation's largest food manufacturer, General Foods. It started in 1925 with the acquisition of the Jello Company; followed by Ingleheart Brothers Flour Mill and the Minute Tapioca

The Road to Wellville

IF YOU have the slightest ambition to " Do things " in this world, to enjoy the keenest delights of Power, Money, Fame, and the perfect poise of Health, by all means get your feet on the " Road to Wellville."

Published by
POSTUM CEREAL CO., LTD.,
Battle Creek, Mich.
COPYRIGHTED

Early packages of Grape Nuts and other Post products came packed with a little pamphlet called The Road to Wellville. *It contained a succinct account of C.W. Post's mental healing philosophy, which he had earlier published as* I Am Well. *Courtesy, Larry B. Massie*

Company in 1926; Franklin Baker Coconut, Walter Baker Chocolate, and Log Cabin Syrup in 1927; Maxwell House Coffee and Calumet Baking Powder in 1928; and Birds Eye, Diamond Crystal Salt, and Certo in 1929. In the final year of the Roaring Twenties the Postum Company became a division of General Foods.

Post's original turn-of-the-century success which developed into the huge food conglomerate inspired a rash of competition in Battle Creek. The city had never been short on speculators quick to emulate a good thing. Post's speedy spring to riches provided a shining example to others who might dream up a cereal recipe variation, coin a catchy brand name, and soon have buildings named in their honor. As one species of gambler staked his all on the Alaskan goldfields, others rushed to pan their fortunes out of golden fields of grain. Battle Creek joined the 20th century in the grip of a breakfast food mania.

During the first decade of the century approximately 80 different brands of breakfast cereal made at least a temporary Battle Creek debut. Proprietors started with wheat, corn, rice, oats, or combinations thereof, chopped 'em, mushed 'em, compressed 'em, impregnated 'em, baked 'em, and flaked 'em into every possible form, added exotic flavorings, and tried them on the public taste buds. They spent countless sleepless nights dreaming up clever packaging gimmicks and novel brand names. There was Grain-O, Grape Sugar Flakes,

Malted Zweiback, Malt-Too, My Food, Flak-Ota, Cocoa Cream Flakes, Cereola, and Egg-O-See. Most tasted about the way they sounded. Frumenta tasted pretty good, but the sharp-edged flakes cut consumers' mouths. A popular joke of the period claimed that Michigan lumbermen created the cereal industry to make use of all the sawdust from their mills.

A homesick Buckeye invented a cooked oat cereal, spelled dear old Akron backwards, and called it Norka. W.H. Hamilton threw down his apron at the grocery store to produce Per-Fo, short for perfect food. A local druggist, John E. Linihan, left his mortar and pestle to spray wheat flakes with apple jelly and stake his future on Cero-Fruto. In 1902 Linihan assured consumers that his apple-flavored flakes were not only "crisp, delicious, and toothsome," but somehow they "made pure blood and a clear brain." Neil S. Phelps took time from his publishing and sanatorium operations to go into partnership with an ex-piano salesman, A.C. Wisner, and market Malta-Vita. The Battle Creek boom lured a couple of young mechanics from Kalamazoo who launched the Korn Krisp Company. They had a good brand name, but they left too much oil in their malt-flavored flakes, and the product grew moldy on grocery shelves. The Fuller brothers gave up on cornflakes and returned to tinkering with transmissions. All but a few of the other cereal-bowl aspirants met a similar fate.

The Hygienic Food Company grew out of the get-rich-quick dreams of W.I. Fell, an Ypsilanti clothing store operator. Fell's variation on the cereal theme was Mapl-Flakes. According to his 1902 advertising, the mighty University of Michigan football team crunched Mapl-Flakes "by the barrel." The team managed a winning record that year, but Mapl-Flakes did not. Hygienic Food Company assets soon passed to Cero-Fruto, which gave up the ghost to the Armour Grain Company. Finally the Ralston Purina Company, one of the few to survive, bought out Armour.

University of Michigan training tables evidently comprised a likely test grounds for Battle Creek cereals. In 1903 Wolverine trackmen vouched for Malto-Flakes, "the rational food for men and women who wish to eat for strength." University of Michigan fans also learned that "athletes who eat Bordeau Flakes

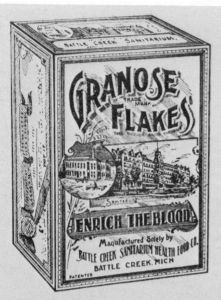

Something Good

To Eat,
and Easy to Digest.

GRANOSE

A new cereal preparation made from the choicest wheat, by a process which retains all the elements of the grain. By combining the processes of digestion, cooking, and roasting, by the use of special machinery, the wheat is brought into the form of delicate flakes, in which the bran is thoroughly disintegrated, and the starch largely converted into dextrin, and thus made ready for solution by the digestive juice and for prompt assimilation.

GRANOSE

Is crisp, delicious, appetizing, and digests quicker than any other cereal preparation. It clears off the tongue, rids the stomach of germs, and cures constipation.

It is unique; an incomparable food. Babies thrive upon it.

BATTLE CREEK SANITARIUM HEALTH FOOD COMPANY,
Battle Creek, Mich.

Above: An 1898 edition of John Harvey Kellogg's popular medical treatise, Ladies' Guide in Health and Disease *carried an advertisement for his Granose Flakes. Dr. Kellogg marketed his invention, the world's first wheat flake, as a health food. Courtesy, Larry B. Massie*

Above, right: The Grape Sugar Flake production room demonstrates the unsanitary conditions that caused the demise of all but a few of the more than 80 breakfast cereal companies that sprang up during the turn-of-the-century Battle Creek cereal boom. Courtesy, Michigan Room, Willard Public Library

never get stale." The cereal's namesake, Jesse D. Bordeau, had learned the business as bakery foreman at Dr. Kellogg's Sanitarium Food Company. He defected and passed his secrets to the Malta-Vita people. Next he set up his own business, the Bordeau Food Company, where he "cooked and crushed the whole wheat berry" to come up with a "pre-digested food," Boston Brown Flakes.

Probably the strangest cereal concoction served up to University of Michigan athletes was the brainchild of a mysterious Chicago entrepreneur, Dr. V.C. Price. Price caught the cereal fever in 1903 and set up in an old water-powered mill at Yorkville, a hamlet between Battle Creek and Kalamazoo. He capitalized on the Cereal City's fame and Kalamazoo's reputation as the Celery City to come up with Triabita, a celery-flavored cereal. Price soaked wheat kernels in a celery-flavored solution, flattened, toasted, and boxed them under the label of a little girl spooning down the mixture, framed between wheat sheaves and celery stalks. Price assured consumers that his "wheat flakes celery food" was not only "endorsed by dietetic experts, pure food manufacturers, and

chemists," but "used exclusively at the Varsity training table." While the unpleasant-sounding mixture made "a perfect food for all classes of people of all ages," the Price Cereal Food Company survived less than a year.

As scores of imaginative adventurers swooped into Battle Creek to try their recipes for cereal success, a local boy sensed an opportunity to sell a little real estate. Benjamin F. Morgan set up the World's Fare Food Company, Ltd., and dubbed his product Golden Manna. In 1902 Morgan advertised his yellow meal to be "vitalizing, health giving, crisp, dainty, delicious, appetizing, and the invalid's delight." It was also, Morgan announced in a burst of alliteration, "Battle Creek's best builder of blood, bone, body, brawn, and brain." Most of Golden Manna's advertising, however, centered around the firm's Morgan Park automobile. The three-seater with a fringed top led Labor Day parades and putted around the city scaring horses. Packed in every package of Golden Manna was a ticket good for a free ride in the novel contraption. Sightseers piled into the vehicle and took a nice leisurely drive out to the newly platted Morgan Park addition for the sales pitch.

In addition to incipient cereal makers, Battle Creek's breakfast bonanza drew a variety of beverage manufacturers who catered to the victims of coffeeism and brain fag. By the turn of the century the city boasted six firms in production of health drinks. When Lewis G. Stevenson, Adlai's father, launched the Javril Coffee Company, his employees had to camp out on the pastureland surrounding the plant because of the housing shortage brought by the boom. C.W. Post viewed these imitators as interlopers. Drawing an image from his Texas days, Post declared them "buzzards roosting on a fence watching for some choice bones to lick." C.W.'s competitors sold their products for 15 cents, a dime less than Postum. Post "concluded to twist the wrist of some of these pirates." He organized a new company, named its product Monk's Brew, designed flashy packages, and filled them with Postum. Monk's Brew retailed at five cents, less than the cost of production. When his competition "died promptly and violently on all sides," Post withdrew Monk's Brew, and the entire market lay in Postum's lap.

But the upshot of the frenzied excitement over breakfast cereals was that Dr. Kellogg, whose health food inventions had founded the boom, was being left in the lurch. By 1902 his Sanitas Nut Food Company was in the red. Kellogg's reluctance to spend money on advertising compounded the problem. He relied predominantly on the pages of his own journal, *Good Health*, to spread the message. Beyond his ingrained frugality he did not want to further antagonize his medical peers by lending his name to a commercial venture. The profession already held some uncomplimentary opinions about the unorthodox procedures at the Sanitarium. Dr. Kellogg also stubbornly clung to the philosophy that his products' attraction lay in their therapeutic value. In an 1897 advertisement featuring a full view of the Sanitarium, Kellogg urged, "If you have been looking for a reliable food cure for constipation and indigestion try Granose." He mentioned as an afterthought that his wheat flakes were "crisp, delicate, and delicious."

Kellogg had invented Granose, the world's first flaked breakfast food, in 1894. When an elderly patient broke her false teeth on some zwieback he prescribed, and demanded restitution, he concluded, "we ought to have a ready cooked food which would not break people's teeth." Kellogg puzzled over the problem, and characteristically the solution came during a dream. He remembered getting up the next morning, boiling up some wheat in his wife's experimental kitchen, rolling it out into a thin dough, scraping it off the bread board, and baking it into a crust in the oven.

Dr. Kellogg's normally indelible memory

failed to record the part played by his brother Will during the experiment. But that was characteristic of their fraternal relationship. Born April 7, 1860, in Battle Creek, the seventh son of a seventh child, William Keith Kellogg had not enjoyed a very lucky childhood. Three of his siblings died and he himself had barely survived a bout of the ague, as malaria was called on the Michigan frontier. The vicissitudes of large family life, a stern Adventist upbringing, hard work, and long hours in his father's broom factory left their imprint on W.K.'s personality. "As a boy I never learned to play," he later remarked. One Adventist schoolteacher, who taught with the bible in one hand and rod in the other, thought Kellogg dim-witted because he had difficulty reading from the blackboard. Not until he was 20 years old did Kellogg discover that the problem lay in his near-sightedness. He grew into a shy, taciturn adult who found it almost impossible to smile.

At the age of 14, Will Kellogg went on the road as a broom salesman. Two years later he moved to Kalamazoo to work at his brother Albert's broom factory. When that went broke, he camped on Albert's front porch until he got

"Post's Addition," C.W. Post's turn-of-the-century suburban development for his workers, contained row after row of dwellings such as this popular Queen Anne-style house. Post's workers could buy six- to eight-room dwellings at the development at prices ranging from $800 to $3,000. Courtesy, Post Division, General Foods Corporation

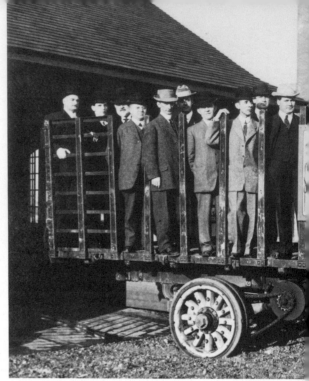

Above: *Early techniques in cereal-making relied heavily on manual labor. Here a Kellogg Company employee, in 1911, removes pans of grain from cookers where they were steamed under pressure for three hours at 360 degrees. Copyright, 1984, courtesy, Kellogg Company*

his back wages. In 1879 Kellogg tried the rough-and-tumble life of Texas, but, sickened by the open sewers that ran alongside Dallas streets, he was back in Michigan within a year. In 1880 he picked up a degree from Parsons' Business College in Kalamazoo, finishing the year-long course in three months. Following graduation, 20-year-old Kellogg married a neighbor girl, Ella Osborn Davis, and armed with his business diploma secured a job working for his brother at the Sanitarium for six dollars a week.

Throughout the following quarter-century, as the Battle Creek Sanitarium won worldwide fame, flamboyant Dr. Kellogg reaped the glory while his unassuming brother worked behind the scenes to keep the institution solvent. W.K. Kellogg never received a distinct title, but his duties ranged from janitor to business manager. He put in up to 120 hours a week, keeping books, securing financing for the doctor's diverse schemes, interviewing prospective patients, answering correspondence, and arranging funerals for those who did not make it through the hydropathic regimen. W.K. shaved the doctor and blacked his shoes, ran the complicated "magic lantern" that projected lurid slides of diseased organs to accompany the doctor's lectures, and sometimes jogged along discussing business while his older brother took his constitutional on a bicycle. After three-and-a-half years he received a raise of one dollar a week, but never earned more

than $87 a month. He confided in his 1884 diary, "I feel kind of blue. Am afraid that I will always be a poor man the way things look now." In the early 1890s Dr. Kellogg offered him 25 percent of the profits on any of his subscription books he could sell, and W.K. added that concern to his 15-hour work day.

W.K. assisted his brother and offered important suggestions during the experiments that resulted in Granose. The doctor tried running boiled wheat paste through a set of rollers, and the wheat stuck to the rolls. W.K. attached a paper-knife blade, which peeled the flakes off, but the substance was still a failure. They accidentally learned the secret when they used a batch of cooked wheat that had been left to stand for several days. The mixture was moldy, but to their surprise one large thin flake for each wheat berry came off the rollers. They had inadvertently discovered the process of tempering necessary to equalize the moisture content throughout the wheat. When baked, the resulting flakes proved crisp and tasty. The doctor wanted to rub the flakes through a screen to make a crumb-like texture, but W.K. advised him to leave them whole. Sanitarium patients liked the new food, and the Kelloggs began commercial production of Granose in a little barn behind the institution. To meet the demand for the novel food, the operation ran 24 hours a day to produce 113,400 pounds of flakes the first year. Management of the newly formed Sanitarium Health Food Company naturally fell to W.K.

In 1898 W.K. began experimenting on his own, using corn instead of wheat. The initial results using the whole corn kernels yielded

had not authorized it W.K. had to pay for it out of his own pocket. Spurred by Post's rapid rise to wealth and convinced that a great future lay in his new recipe for cornflakes, early in 1902 W.K. told his brother he was quitting. But before he could get away, the Sanitarium burned down, and W.K. gallantly agreed to stay on to help rebuild.

As he went about the task of refinancing the new Sanitarium building, W.K. began asserting his ideas about selling cereal. The doctor had prohibited sweetening in the flakes, but during another of his European tours, W.K. incorporated cane sugar into the recipe and developed a tastier product. When the doctor returned, he "had a fit," but the sugar stayed. Against the doctor's wishes W.K., in concert with a young advertising genius, Arch Shaw, began a mass advertising campaign to promote the Sanitas Flakes for their appetite appeal. W.K. reasoned that the biggest share of the market lay not with the dyspeptic but with well people. By 1903 newspaper advertisements, streetcar signs, window displays, and billboards promoted Toasted Corn Flakes, "A breakfast treat—that makes you eat." Concerned with his medical standing and preoccupied with his primary project, the Sanitarium, Dr. Kellogg grew increasingly troubled over cornflakes.

In late 1905 W.K. approached the doctor with a proposition to separate the cornflake business from the Sanitas Nut Food Company

Left: In 1912 Kellogg Company sales managers posed for a publicity photograph aboard the company's new chain-driven Packard delivery truck. The vehicle's hard-rubber tires guaranteed a bumpy ride. Copyright, 1984, courtesy, Kellogg Company

thick, rather tasteless flakes. But Dr. Kellogg named them Sanitas Toasted Corn Flakes, put them up in a blue package carrying an illustration of the Sanitarium building, and promoted them as a health food. Whole carloads came back, spoiled. The product was too moist to keep on the shelf. A few years later W.K. tried corn grits, the "sweetheart of the corn," added malt flavoring, and came up with a crisp tasty flake that stayed fresh.

About that time "J.H.'s flunkey" decided he'd had enough of the doctor's treatment. An incident that helped make up his mind occurred in 1900. While the doctor was away gallivanting through Europe, W.K. built a new $50,000 brick production plant. When the doctor returned, he informed W.K. that since he

Below: Women workers paid close attention to their tasks as they boxed Kellogg's® Whole Wheat Biscuits during the early 1930s. Kellogg's offered a novel concept in packaging, a cellophane window which allowed consumers to view the actual product. Copyright, 1984, courtesy, Kellogg Company

"Excuse me—I know what I want, and I want what I asked for—TOASTED CORN FLAKES—Good day"

The package of the genuine bears this signature

W. K. Kellogg

In 1911 artist Henry Hutt created a determined Gibsonesque young lady who knew what she wanted. Copyright, 1984, courtesy, Kellogg Company

and create a separate corporation under his management. On February 19, 1906, the Battle Creek Toasted Corn Flake Company was incorporated with a majority of the stock going to Dr. Kellogg. Securing financial backing from Charles D. Bolen, a St. Louis insurance man, W.K. started out with about one-third of the stock in the new company. The doctor distributed a portion of his stock to Sanitarium staff in lieu of a pay raise and left for his annual pilgrimage to Europe. When he returned he was no longer in command of the Corn Flake Company. W.K. had patiently wheedled enough stock from the Sanitarium staff to stand as majority shareholder. The 46-year-old underling had pledged all his life's savings in the company to start a new chapter in his career.

The Battle Creek Toasted Corn Flake Company went into production in the same rickety old building on Bartlett Street where the Hygienic Food Company had gone broke manufacturing Mapl-Flakes. The initial output was 33 cases a day. Taking a leaf from C.W. Post, Kellogg sank one-third of his working capital into a full-page advertisement in *Ladies Home Journal*. Kellogg used reverse psychology by informing the magazine's six million readers that they could not have his cornflakes because he was so behind in orders. Naturally the public wanted what they could not have, and they clamored for cornflakes. Kellogg expanded production facilities to a portion of the Sanitas plant and the old Norka building. Within six months output swelled to 2,900 cases a day. By the end of 1906 Kellogg had spent $90,000 for advertising, nearly all his profit and roughly three times his initial working capital.

The Bartlett Street plant burned to the ground on July 4, 1907. Within a month Kellogg secured a new site on Porter Street, north of Post's "white city," which allowed him access to both the Grand Trunk and Michigan Central railroads. Subliminal advertising campaigns urging housewives to "give the grocer a wink and see what you get" and to open the door "when the bell rings three times" distributed boxes of free cornflakes and produced an avalanche of new orders. In 1909 the renamed Kellogg's Toasted Corn Flake Company sold one million cases of packages labeled "none genuine without this signature—W.K. Kellogg."

Avant-garde advertising techniques comprised an important element in the company's success. While C.W. Post married his secretary, W.K. Kellogg chose one of his to portray the "sweetheart of the corn" on his cereal labels. A wholesome-looking beauty hugging corn stalks remained a favorite Kellogg advertising symbol for generations. By 1911 Kellogg's advertising budget reached one million dollars a year. Massive electric billboards blinked across New York City and Chicago skylines, nationally circulated magazines featured innovative color advertisements, and children sent envelopes bulging with box tops for appealing cereal premiums. In 1932, at the depth of the Depression, Kellogg doubled his advertising budget, and company sales continued to rise. By 1940 the company had spent approximately $100 million for advertising.

As W.K.'s cornflake empire grew by leaps and bounds, and the jack-of-all-trades Sanitarium worker who thought he would always be a poor man became a millionaire, resentment pent up over a quarter-century of apprenticeship and the doctor's continued imperiousness brought a widening rift in their fraternal relationship. Dr. Kellogg's egoism led him to underestimate his younger brother's capabilities and to assume he himself would stay in command. When the Battle Creek Toasted Corn Flake Company separated from the Sanitas Nut Food Company, W.K. received a salary of $250 a month for managing the operation. The doctor insisted on their usual 75 percent-25 percent arrangement, and for several months W.K. suffered the humiliation of endorsing his paycheck over to his brother who doled back 25 percent of the amount. When W.K.'s advertising daring made Kellogg's Corn Flakes famous, the doctor assumed he was the Kellogg referred to.

A long series of legal battles over use of the Kellogg name intensified their hostility into hatred. For more than three decades the brothers seized any opportunity to hurt each other's business or reputation. In 1943 when Dr. Kellogg fought his last battle to prevent an Adventist takeover of the Sanitarium, W.K. did all in his power to support the church hierarchy. Just prior to his death in December, Dr. Kellogg penned a conciliatory note to his estranged brother, acknowledging that he had wronged him in the past. But before the message was delivered, the doctor had gone.

While W.K. had a vindictive facet to his character, the final tally of his life's ledger reveals an overwhelming kindness and devotion to assisting his fellow human being. Old friends down on their luck received a visit from W.K. culminating in a handshake that carried a finely folded $20 bill. Others received mysterious phone calls notifying them that doctor bills or mortgages had been anonymously paid up.

The passing of the last of Battle Creek's great cereal entrepreneurs, W.K. Kellogg, in 1951 concluded an amazing chapter in the city's and America's history. But Dr. J.H. Kellogg, the inventive crusader, C.W. Post, the innovative

promoter, and W.K. Kellogg, the hard-working realist, left a far-reaching legacy mirrored in part by the factories, homes, institutions, and spirit of today's Battle Creek, "the Cereal Capital of the World."

Above: *In 1907 one of Kellogg Company's earliest advertisements, which appeared in nationally circulated journals, featured a little girl hungrily awaiting her* Kellogg's Corn Flakes.® *Copyright, 1984, courtesy, Kellogg Company*

Left: *In 1912 Kellogg Company constructed the largest electric sign in the world atop the Mecca Building in New York City's Times Square. Eighty tons of structural iron went into the 106-feet-wide by 80-feet-high colossus. Copyright, 1984, courtesy, Kellogg Company*

CHAPTER VI

Made in Battle Creek

Battle Creek boomed into the 20th century. The longest high-tension wire in the world brought electricity 46 miles when the switch was thrown on May 19, 1900, at the Allegan Dam. The Phelps Sanatorium, built in 1900, became the largest fieldstone building in the United States. The city renamed the three "Canal" streets Madison, Monroe, and State. Local citizens organized the town's first golf club in 1900. The census taker counted 18,563 people that year, one of whom, E.C. Adams, drove an automobile. Two thousand others worked in 76 factories, the largest of which still made threshing machines. But the state "factory inspector" reported the next year that the city had become the mecca "where searchers for pure food journey." C.W. Post headed the cereal excitement in those days, beginning with "Postum," a cereal coffee substitute in 1895. By 1901 people called his 16 buildings and the workers' homes around them "Postumville." Before long they would call his works "the White City." An advertising genius, Post put his faith in Battle Creek, building the town's first seven-story "skyscraper" in 1900 and the great Post Tavern the next year.

Newcomers flocked to town attracted by the highest factory wages in the state. People worked hard in those days. The 10-hour day and 6-day week were common everywhere, though some cereal firms like the Battle Creek Pure Food Company worked round the clock, seven days a week. Factory inspectors reported the great disparity between wages paid men and women, though "each sex may be engaged at the same occupation and are working the same number of hours per day." In 1904 the old and weary saying, "another day, another dollar" held true for the city's 417 "factory girls," while men earned nearly twice that.

Local factory workers averaged $557 a year in 1904. Wages varied little in the latter part of the 19th century. A young man might enter the work force at $1.50 a day and labor all his life for little more. Yet prices remained stable as well. Market basket prices in 1904 might include:

flour	*$5.20 barrel*
firewood	*3.00 cord*
coal	*6.00 ton*
house rent	*6.15 month*

rocking chair	*4.00*
butter	*.25 pound*
eggs	*.18 dozen*
ham	*.18 pound*
sirloin	*.15 pound*
pork	*.15 pound*
chicken	*.16 pound*
Uneeda biscuits	*.05 box*
oranges	*.25 peck*
cigar	*.05*
tooth extraction	*.25*
gingham	*.10 yard*

We can better understand the value of such items in terms of the time it took to pay for them. A man might work an hour for a dozen eggs or a pound of ham and slightly less for beef, pork, or chicken. A bushel of potatoes cost the better part of a day, and a laborer might work three or four days for a ton of coal. Four days' wages paid a month's rent, and not much longer covered a year's property taxes. Women worked twice as long for the same results.

City life drew large numbers of working women, who outnumbered men in every age from 15 to 50. According to one survey in 1902, the average working woman was 24, and 8 out of 10 were single. Most worked 50 weeks in the year, 10 hours a day, for $.92 a day. Two out of three lived at home, and nearly 90 percent said they had no one but themselves to support. Two out of three said they spent all they earned. Many women boarded, for there were few apartments or "flats" as they were called. Most workers lived in detached dwellings much like their neighbors.

With 22,213 people, Battle Creek ranked as Michigan's seventh-largest city in 1904. The Michigan Bureau of Labor inspectors reported, "there are a number of model factories, which compare favorably with the best in the State, and the employees' interests well looked after." Post and Nichols & Shepard offered homes to their married workers on easy terms. The 1904 census found local housing the most spacious of any industrial community with an average of 4.1 people per dwelling.

Battle Creek grew faster than any other industrial center in the state at the turn of the century. Between 1900 and 1904 the number of manufacturing establishments increased by 58 percent to 120. Capital invested grew by 80 per-

cent, and the number of workers by two-thirds. The value of Battle Creek's products nearly doubled; and wages, stable for decades, suddenly shot up 92 percent, nearly twice the state average. By 1904 corporations controlled 40 percent of the town's 120 factories. The days when old John Nichols worked in the plant beside his men were long gone. Nine of ten factory hands now worked for the corporations. In fact, 70 percent of the labor force worked in 15 percent of the factories—the highest concentration in the state. Four of every ten made their way each morning to the three largest firms, who paid nearly half the town's payroll. The 18 largest companies accounted for 85 percent of the value of all products.

Cereal contributed its share to these statistics, with the Post Company rapidly pulling away. But the town's largest employer was still the venerable Nichols & Shepard threshing machine company with 296 workers. American Steam Pump Company ranked third behind Post, with Advance Thresher and Duplex Printing Press next. Each of these firms built a solid market for products that carried the name of Battle Creek around the world. The two implement makers regularly shipped trainloads of threshers all over the country. The pump makers specialized in heavy-duty equipment for oil wells, mines, and factories around the world. Duplex marketed a line of presses that revolutionized newspaper printing.

Battle Creek's boom continued year after year. By 1907 the total number of workers increased 19 percent, but the half-dozen largest factories grew 75 percent. Post went from 261 to 618, Advance from 180 to 467, Duplex from 148 to 246. Taylor Brothers candy factory grew from 75 to 200. But for all its bustle and hustle and bigness, Battle Creek offered opportunities for newcomers as well.

Relatively few immigrants made their way to Battle Creek, where 77 percent of the population were sons or daughters of native-born parents (compared to 12 percent in Ironwood). Of all Calhoun County's 50,000 residents, only 20 had come from Italy. One of these 20, Albert Ratti, worked as an alley tender in Battle Creek. He wrote in glowing terms to his brother Alex in Ann Arbor, telling him of "the little town with the big industries" and urging him to move.

Facing page: Nineteenth century pump maker Amos Mills worked in this old wooden shop on "Canal Street" from 1880 to 1900, but such small industry was increasingly unusual by the early 1900s when modern factories dominated the local economy. Courtesy, Michigan Room, Willard Public Library

Alex Ratti's move to Battle Creek began in the Italian hill towns years before. He and his cousin Achilles left home in 1871. One went to Rome to study; the other came alone to America at the age of 16. Alex Ratti quickly learned what it meant to be an immigrant. With a nickel in his pocket and no English, he found a place to stay with a German family, newcomers too. He took a meal now and then at a soup kitchen while he hunted a job and learned the language. Ratti tried his hand at everything—farm labor, gandy-dancing on the railroads, working with the circus. He came to Detroit as a fortune-teller, but stayed to learn the candy-making business. He saved his money and earned his citizenship. When it came time to marry, he went back to Italy for his bride and returned to open a candy store. He prospered as a "confectioner" over the years, buying properties in Pontiac and Ann Arbor. When his first wife died, he went back again to his home village and married Louisa Sinelli in 1898. She returned with him to Ann Arbor, where they opened an ice cream parlor near the University of Michigan campus. By this time two of Alex's brothers had come to America—one to Battle Creek. Alex decided to visit the "Cereal City" and measure its opportunities for himself. In 1906 he took a job as a food worker with the Michigan Central Railroad and came to Battle Creek. Prospects looked promising. He met the Post family and rented space from them at 95 West Michigan, just a few doors down from the big new Post Tavern. There he opened the town's first ice cream parlor.

The next years were exciting ones for the whole Ratti family. The ice cream and candy business kept everyone busy. With his children growing up, Ratti bought a house at 15 Adams Street. Then in 1912 he bought a lot just down the street on Michigan Avenue. There the masons worked busily through 1913, putting up the 39-foot double store called the Alex Ratti Block. He rented both shops at first. Between them a narrow staircase led to a second-floor hotel.

Alex went back to Italy for his health in 1922. The next year the ice cream parlor burned. The family moved down the street to 115 but decided a few months later to give up making ice cream. They began a haberdashery in 1923, and it is still in business.

Ratti's health continued to fail, and his two sons, George and Alex, Jr., took on more responsibilities. When the elder Ratti died in 1927, Alex, 26, and George, 24, continued to call the firm Ratti & Sons. Their mother, Louisa, took over management of The Victoria Hotel at 115 1/2 West Michigan and continued to operate it until 1940. George branched out for a time in the late 1920s, running a billiard parlor across the street along with Peter Valmassoi, Sam Bombassei, and Dominick Zonda. He married and lived at the store for a time. Alex, Jr., remained a bachelor.

Alex Ratti, Jr., went to Italy himself in 1929, hoping to meet his father's cousin. He remembers seeing him pass by in a corridor, then stop and come back to look closely—"I knew he thought we must be related somehow." Then the cousin turned and resumed his walk, because "the Pope didn't talk to people in those days." Alex Ratti's young cousin had indeed gone on to study. Achilles Ambrose Damien Ratti had risen to papal librarian by 1914 and was named Pope Pius XI in 1922. He headed the Catholic Church until 1939.

Alex Ratti built only one of many new downtown buildings. Construction activity continued all around the site of his block. A grant from the Charles Willard family led to the new Willard Library in 1904. W.K. Kellogg survived a disastrous fire in 1907 and began his new Battle Creek Toasted Corn Flake plant. A $15,000 post office was finished the same year. The Methodists completed a big new church in 1908. The city built a new $300,000 high school in 1909, and C.W. Post added a handsome 10-story addition to the Tavern in 1912. Battle Creek became one of the first communities to adopt the city commission form of government in 1913. The same year saw construction begin on a brand new city hall, celebrating its prominence as "the best-known city of its size in the country."

More than 34,000 people lived in Battle Creek by 1917, well over half the population of the county. Nine thousand eighty-six worked in 245 industries, roughly a third of them in the 10 largest factories—1,111 at Post Cereal alone. A list of local products included: "threshing machines, portable engines, health foods, stoves, oven racks, paper roofing, tables, paper, boilers, canvas gloves, electrical goods, wire

Right: *The renovated upper stories of older business blocks retain something of their 19th century exuberance along the downtown mall. Courtesy, Peter J. Schmitt*

Below: *"Circa: Gateway to the Future," a 1982 steel sculpture by Michael Calligan, stands at the new Transportation Center and symbolizes the city's hopes. Courtesy, Peter J. Schmitt*

82

Above left: *Water sports have been an important part of Battle Creek's summer fun ever since pioneers first relaxed at Goguac Lake in the 1860s. Courtesy, JMT, Inc.*

Above: *Thousands of visitors watched as Battle Creek hosted the Fifth World Hot Air Balloon Championship in 1981. Since then the city has become a center for competitive ballooning. Courtesy, JMT, Inc.*

Left: *The history and prosperity of Battle Creek can be seen in its sky-line. Courtesy, Peter J. Schmitt*

Left: *This postcard view of the main thoroughfare in 1940 shows the city much as it was in the early 1980s, except for the pedestrian mall, which opened in 1974. Courtesy, Michigan Room, Willard Public Library*

Facing page, top: *Battle Creek wound quietly through the town in this 1911 postcard view. By this time it was no longer an important power source for industry. Courtesy, Michigan Room, Willard Public Library*

Left: *Battle Creek was proud of its motorized fire equipment, shown in this 1914 postcard. The fire department bought its first motor truck in 1911, at a cost of $5,500. Courtesy, Michigan Room, Willard Public Library*

Facing page, bottom: *This 1918 postcard suggests the impressiveness of Battle Creek Sanitarium buildings. The Sanitarium Annex shown here was originally built in 1900 as the Phelps Sanitarium, and has been called the largest flagstone structure in the U.S. C.W. Post bought it in 1904, and J.H. Kellogg bought it in 1914 as the headquarters for the "Race Betterment Foundation." At one time it also served as a dormitory for the old Battle Creek College. Courtesy, Michigan Room, Willard Public Library*

VOTES for WOMEN

GOOD FRIENDS

Said the Elephant to his friend the Giraffe,   If only I had such a fine, long neck,
"Your taster's so long it makes me laugh.   I'd eat Kellogg's Corn Flakes by the peck.

QUEER FELLOWS

If you wish to see something queer,   Change their feet, too, try it and see
Put other heads on the Cow, Horse and Deer.   How very funny they all will be.

The Home Plate

W. K. Kellogg

LOOK FOR THIS SIGNATURE

Above, left: *Kellogg Company's early advertising often utilized contemporary social issues. Votes For Women® did not become a national reality until ratification of the 19th Amendment in 1920, but this 1914 advertisement implied the new freedom provided American housewives through the availability of Kellogg's® ready-to-eat breakfast foods. Copyright, 1984, courtesy, Kellogg Company*

Left: *A 1912 Kellogg Company advertisement featured the great American pastime and a clever play on words:* Sliding Into Home Plate. *In 1911 the company introduced a baseball game that was printed on the inside of Kellogg's Corn Flakes® boxes. Copyright, 1984, courtesy, Kellogg Company*

Facing page: *A series of ads depicting Boy Scouts eating breakfast at camp appeared in the official Boy Scout publication, Boys Life, in 1928. The backdrop for these ads was Camp T. Ben Johnson, located at Sherman Lake, near Augusta, Michigan. Copyright, 1984, courtesy, Kellogg Company*

Above: *In 1909 the Kellogg Company offered Kellogg's Funny Jungleland® as a cereal premium. The pamphlet contained pages that allowed children to construct unusual animals. Courtesy, Larry B. Massie*

Above and far right: *During the early years of the century the Post Company commissioned artists to paint original illustrations for its nationally circulated advertisements. The original paintings currently hang on the walls of Post's advertising agency. Courtesy, Post Division, General Foods Corporation*

Above, right: *The Kellogg Company offered public tours to promote confidence in its cereal products. Courtesy, Western Michigan University Archives*

Right: *Promotional literature projected a friendly image for the Post cereal empire. Courtesy, Western Michigan University Archives.*

novelties, steam pumps, printing presses, boilers, all kinds of woodworking machinery, flour, albums, shipping tags, account books, sash, doors and blinds, carriages, wagons, paper folding boxes, confectionery, extracts, brass goods, furniture, printing ink, electric appliances, railroad cars and engines, etc."

Battle Creekers read three daily papers, drank water from a $300,000 municipal system, and visited any of 10 different parks on the trolley or any of three interurban lines. The fire department had motorized equipment and the police department, automobiles. There were now 110 miles of roads, 20 of them paved, and 52 miles of sewers.

Battle Creek's building boom paled in comparison to the excitement that struck the town in 1917. The federal government chose a site just west of town for the military training center named after a Michigan boy—George Armstrong Custer. The government moved quickly, signing a construction contract in June, securing 10,000 acres of farmland near the old village of Harmonia, and readying some 2,000 buildings for the 50,000 men expected to attend what promoters were calling "the University of Democracy." Ads for workers cried, "Bring your saw and hammer and get a job!" and men came from all over the Midwest, along with 4,000 carloads of material. Major General Joseph Dickman arrived on August 26, and the first 13 trainees 10 days later. The $8 million Camp Custer was declared officially complete on December 5, just half a year after the first rumors surfaced. It included training grounds, barracks, a 3,000-seat auditorium, a base hospital, seven YMCA buildings, and a $750,000 heating plant.

Camp Custer carried on through the next several months—then tragedy struck on September 29, 1918, when the first soldier fell ill with Spanish influenza. In 10 days 6,817 men went to the hospital. Local newspapers counted as many as 674 deaths and then stopped reporting. Battle Creek residents did what they could to help camp doctors, and the epidemic ran its course as the war ended.

As peacetime returned, Alex Ratti kept five people busy in his ice cream parlor, one of 10 "confectionery" stores in town. The Michigan Bureau of Labor reported 410 men and 523 women working in the city's 128 stores and shops. Of these, 16 companies counted more than 10 employees. Except for Bock-Walker hardware and E.C. Fisher books and stationery, these were all clothing and "department" stores, led by Toeller-Grant with 70 workers and Schroeder Brothers with 50. Thirty-four people worked at S.S. Kresge and 29 at F.W. Woolworth. Most women still worked for less than two dollars a day, while men made nearly four.

Battle Creek boasted six hotels staffed by 173 people. One hundred and twenty-eight worked at the Post Tavern, "known favorably from ocean to ocean." Among hospitals, the Battle Creek Sanitarium then ranked as the largest facility of its kind in the world.

Two-thirds of Calhoun County's industry was centered in Battle Creek by 1919. Eleven thousand, one hundred and twenty-seven people worked for 238 companies, half of them for the six largest firms, which included:

Advance-Rumely, farm machinery *1,454*
Kellogg Toasted Corn Flake Company,
    cereal *1,098*
Postum Cereal Company, cereal *989*
Grand Trunk Railway, engine repairing ... *912*
Nichols & Shepard, threshing machines *667*
Rich Steel Products, small tools *491*

Men earned $4.06 a day for a 55-hour week. Women averaged $2.56. Of the companies reporting their power sources, 149 used electricity, 36 steam, and 4 continued to tap the waters of Battle Creek.

Henry Ford would report in his autobiography that his own experiments might be traced to Nichols & Shepard's early self-propelled threshers. Local auto ownership increased from one in 1900 to 180 in 1910, and now 17 firms sold or serviced automobiles. In 1918 Standard Oil began building the familiar porte cochere gas stations where gravity pumps, their glass cylinders filled with amber liquid expanding in the sunshine, awaited customers along the city's busy streets.

The city grew by 43 percent between 1910 and 1920, ranking 12th in Michigan. One person in 10 could be called "foreign born"— chiefly from Scotland, Ireland, or Northern Europe. Battle Creek continued to call itself a "city of homes." On the average, workers were less crowded at 3.8 per dwelling than in any other major city. Census takers found nearly twice as many people per dwelling in Detroit, for example.

Old companies grew, and new ones came to town. Clark Equipment, expanding from its home in Buchanan, opened a plant in 1922, eventually taking over the A-B Stove works and producing a variety of industrial and forklift trucks. Ralston-Purina moved into the old Mapl-Flake plant in 1927. Rich Steel Products, makers of small tools in Battle Creek since 1916, was absorbed by Wilcox Motor Parts of Saginaw and Detroit in 1928; two years later the parent company merged in turn with Eaton Axle & Spring Company of Cleveland, Ohio. The Rich plant became Eaton's Valve Division.

Tall buildings gave Battle Creek its dramatic skyline. The Sanitarium began its 15-story tower in 1926, finishing it two years and $4 million later, the same year the city changed its faintly provincial "Main Street" to "Michigan Avenue." The Old Merchant's National Bank celebrated its merger in 1929 by adding 15 stories to the former Old National Bank Building.

W.K. Kellogg began a million-dollar addition to his plant in 1929. When the Depression came, he doubled his advertising and went right on making America's breakfast. He went to the six-hour day in 1930, installing a park and athletic field for his workers and offering special cultural programs. By 1935 the company paid one of the highest wages in the

state—75 cents an hour for a 36-hour week.

Kellogg and others saw to it that new construction continued, despite hard times. In 1930 he finished the 100-room Kellogg Hotel at Washington and Van Buren, which Thomas Hart would purchase and rename "The Hart Hotel" in 1938. He also provided funds for the Ann J. Kellogg School where students needing special education profited from one of the country's first "mainstreaming" projects. The city completed the Washington and Verona schools in 1930. St. Philip's congregation pushed ahead on a new Romanesque church, and work began on the great office tower at McCamly and Michigan the same year.

The city's 43,573 residents celebrated the "Cereal City's" centennial gala in 1931, triumphantly recalling pioneer crafts and pioneer virtues. Some saw parallels between the hard times of the 1830s and their own. But 2,000 men still worked at the Grand Trunk Railroad repair shops, and the cereal companies processed 10 million bushels of wheat and corn each year.

No one could say Battle Creek didn't suffer during the Great Depression. By 1932 twelve hundred local families needed some kind of aid. The city offered a free woodpile for unemployed workers, and hundreds of free garden plots filled all vacant land. People still left town. The census taker found fewer residents in 1940 than in 1930, reversing a trend begun a century earlier. But those who stayed outlasted the worst of times. The town took the slogan "Better Yourself in Battle Creek," and people did. Those who could shared their wealth in community projects.

C.W. Post once told his family that "owners of fortunes have responsibilities to society." His widow, Leila Post Montgomery, was honored as one of the town's principal benefactors in 1926. She had given the city the Battle Creek Country Club's old grounds as a 72-acre arboretum in 1922. She also underwrote the cost of the great new Leila Hospital on North Avenue that opened in 1927. Now, in 1930, she offered to fund a large addition. In all, she gave more than a million dollars to local causes. Post's daughter, prominent Washington socialite Marjorie Merriweather Post, helped many other local projects, including the Battle Creek Symphony and Lakeview Hospital. She

In 1926 huge flags brought a patriotic appearance to West Main Street, now West Michigan Avenue. This view taken from Jefferson West, now Capital Avenue Northeast, captured a traffic cop directing traffic between streetcar tracks. Courtesy, Michigan Room, Willard Public Library

is best remembered for her gift of the C.W. Post Athletic Field, with its track, stadium, and tennis courts considered among the finest in the United States.

W.K. Kellogg organized the Kellogg Foundation in 1930, and through it provided a 2,000-seat auditorium in 1933. The city trucked sand from its excavation to improve the Willard Bathing Beach at Goguac Lake. In 1936 W.K. gave Kellogg Airport to the city. The Kellogg Foundation made other lasting contributions to the quality of life in Battle Creek, working particularly with health and school problems.

In the 1930s government played an increasingly important role. President Franklin Roosevelt acted quickly to reinforce the banking industry with his famous "holiday" in 1933. Local businesses scrambled to meet payrolls, and the Old Merchant's National

Bank did close its doors in June. But if the banks might close, Camp Custer came back to life in April, when Colonel Russell Langdon took charge of the new "mobilizing Woodland Army." The first 2,100 Civilian Conservation Corps recruits arrived April 11, and by April 30 four companies were off to the Manistee and Huron national forests. Thousands of young men passed through Camp Custer over the next months as CCC improvements dotted the landscape.

Nineteen thirty-six saw completion of the most sophisticated sewage plant in the state, and a $200,000 loan from the Public Works Administration helped construction of Battle

Creek General Hospital (now Community Hospital). In 1937 the Veterans Administration facility at Camp Custer added a $300,000 addition, and by 1938 the PWA and WPA were spending one million dollars paving streets and removing streetcar tracks.

The Chamber of Commerce actively sought new industries during the lean years, carrying on negotiations with George Rich as early as 1931. By 1935 Rich was ready to reenter the engine valve field he had left in the 1920s. Rich Manufacturing Company prospered, lasting until 1960 when it was sold to Sterling Aluminum Products. In 1936 the Chamber succeeded again when Weston Biscuits came to town. In 1936 Harold and Ruth Swanson opened Swanson Cookie Company, beginning the "Archway" success story. Eugene McKay bought the old Sanitarium Equipment Company building in 1936, intending to set up a private laboratory. A year later he sold to National Biscuit Company, and "Nabisco" came to Battle Creek.

"Bettering Yourself in Battle Creek" also meant bettering the quality of life in the 1930s. Battle Creek had always been called a "city of homes" where, even in the Depression, 7 out of 10 people lived in their own homes. It was a city of social activities as well. Rotary, Kiwanis, and Exchange clubs met regularly, as did the Merchants Dinner and the Knife and Fork Club for local businessmen. The Athelstan Club provided social contacts and a meeting place for

Above: W.K. Kellogg built his elaborate Tudor home "Eagle Heights" on a 15-acre estate at Gull Lake in 1926. He made it available to the U.S. Coast Guard as a reception center during World War II. Later the W.K. Kellogg Foundation presented it to Michigan State University. Courtesy, W.K. Kellogg Foundation

Left: The parade marshall's gaily decked automobile prepares to lead a Fourth of July Parade in 1930 from the police station at North Division and State streets. Courtesy, Michigan Room, Willard Public Library

In 1931 hordes of citizens turned out to view the parade honoring the centennial of Battle Creek's founding. Here the floats pass by the Post Tavern on Michigan Avenue. Courtesy, Michigan Room, Willard Public Library

Facing page, top: In 1944, while World War II raged, many a Battle Creek serviceman dreamed of life back home where a healthy-looking young woman stood ready to dip five-cent ice cream cones at the S.S. Kresge Five and Dime Store. Courtesy, Michigan Room, Willard Public Library

Facing page, bottom: In 1941 the candy counter at Battle Creek's S.S. Kresge store presented a dream come true for those with a sweet tooth. Huge Amos 'n' Andy, Hershey's, and Dreams candy bars sold at three for a dime, while half a pound of bulk peanut brittle was 10 cents. Courtesy, Michigan Room, Willard Public Library

the "Pagans," one of the town's two community theaters. The "Pagans," organized in 1932, provided a variety of local and national drama, starring Deldee Herman in "Hedda Gabler" in one early success. In 1936 the two theater groups became the Battle Creek Civic Players. Disrupted by World War II, the group reorganized in 1946 as today's Civic Theater. The Battle Creek Symphony, one of the country's oldest, was formed in 1899 under the direction of John Martin, who led it for the next 40 years. In 1930 Battle Creek was the first city in the country to form a community concert series.

By the end of the 1930s, Battle Creek residents had come to terms with adversity. The war in Europe helped revive the economy at home. Signs of war appeared as early as 1939. Orders for war materials increased, and long trains rolled through the city. Camp Custer was enlarged and reactivated as Fort Custer—ready to process 9,000 men a month. The Fifth or "Red Diamond" Division began assembling at Fort Custer as early as January 1941. The Fifth, made up of one-year draftees, was caught by the declaration of war in December and sent without leave to Iceland, where it remained until 1944.

The government spent more than a million dollars enlarging Kellogg Field and paving runways in 1941 and 1942. The field became the Army Air Base in August. That same year the government paid $2,251,000 for the main Sanitarium building, renaming it Percy Jones Hospital and later designating it an amputation center. The army's largest hospital treated some 50,000 veterans in its first four years. W.K. Kellogg Foundation camps at St. Mary's, Pine, and Clear lakes became Coast Guard Training Stations in 1940. Some 5,000 men had passed through these centers by the time they were

closed in 1943. In 1943 the Recruit Reception Center at Fort Custer moved to Illinois, and the first contingent of German prisoners arrived.

Battle Creek joined the rest of the country on a war footing. Historian and journalist Art Middleton estimated that 90 percent of all manufacturing in the city went toward the war effort. Duplex Printing Press made 37 millimeter anti-tank guns, for example, and Nichols & Shepard built fuselage sections for B-17 bombers. Need for manpower increased each year. By 1944 the school board approved half-day sessions so that high school students might work. The board also agreed to pay women teachers as much as men. The city reported that "victory gardens" covered all available land. Many were tended by children as more and more women went to work in defense plants. All through the war people saved paper, scrap, grease, and flattened cans. They followed the old adage, "Use it up, wear it out, make it do," and they looked forward to the end of gasoline cards, ration stamps, and lower speed limits.

By 1945 twelve thousand people from Calhoun County had seen service—294 gold stars hung in area windows, honoring those who would never return. Signs of peace were welcomed everywhere. Commercial airline service resumed in 1945, and the army returned Kellogg Field to city control the next year. Five thousand German prisoners left for home in 1946. New cars appeared in dealers' showrooms, though in short supply. Prices rose, and parking meters were installed on downtown streets. People looked everywhere for peacetime housing. Local builders began 667 homes that year and hundreds more the next.

Temporary inconvenience brought lasting changes as the city welcomed the postwar era with long-overdue public improvements. A flood-control project harnessed the Kalamazoo River after floodwaters poured into the downtown area in 1947. This project culminated in 1961 with the dedication of the present concrete river channel. Most Battle Creek residents were accustomed to unpaved roads and the annual battle with frost heaves. As late as 1950 only 77 of the city's 160 miles of roadway had been paved, but the city soon carried out a massive roadwork program. Thirty-four miles were paved between 1956 and 1958 alone. By 1960 the city boasted 140 miles of paving, and "mud vacation" was a thing of the past. The Battle Creek Gas Company boosted its gas mains to 224 miles, adding 33 miles between 1951 and 1954. A decade later the company began another burst of activity, laying 226 miles of pipe between 1966 and 1971. Other basic improvements included five new bridges over the Kalamazoo in 1958, and the $4 million "Penetrator" connecting the city to Interstate 94 in 1966.

Battle Creek residents caught the postwar enthusiasm for suburban living. People moved away from the city, but the surrounding metropolitan district continued to grow. Battle Creek responded by expanding its city limits wherever possible. But voters generally resisted ambitious annexation proposals, such as the plan to absorb four townships in 1966.

Old landmarks were lost, and new ones appeared in the construction boom. First National Realty Company bought the Central National Bank Tower at McCamly and West Michigan in 1947 and sold it to Wolverine Insurance in 1951. The Wolverine Tower later became the Transamerica Building. The Post Tavern celebrated its 50th anniversary in 1950, but the old walls came down 10 years later; by 1970 the Post Tavern was only a memory.

Battle Creek Community College opened its doors in 1956 with five instructors and 95 students. Two years later taxpayers voted a millage increase, and the Kellogg Foundation offered $2 million to bring about the first buildings on North Avenue. Renamed in 1959, Kellogg Community College grew rapidly. The 166-acre campus provided an attractive learning environment and a wide variety of programs to meet modern community needs. Presently more than 7,000 students register every year.

The Civic Art Center, formed in 1947, joined with an active community theater, the community chorus, and the Battle Creek Symphony Orchestra as the United Arts Council in 1964 with headquarters on the KCC campus.

Union Steam Pump dropped "Steam" from its name in 1959, the year the city celebrated its centennial. Journalist Ross Coller wrote a

Rampaging flood waters left downtown businesses determined to change things in 1947. This view looking east from Division across the Michigan Central railyard suggests the extent of the disaster, which led ultimately to a major government flood-control project completed by 1961. Courtesy, Michigan Room, Willard Public Library

special history commemorating Battle Creek's emergence from a rural trading center to a modern industrial community. Coller found 43 percent of area workers involved in the cereal industry in some way. But heavy industry provided an equally solid foundation, as did a host of smaller manufacturing firms. The V.C. Squier Company, for example, was a nationally known maker of musical instrument strings in business since 1890. Gage Printing Company had been prominent since its founding in 1883. United Steel & Wire marked its 50th anniversary, counting the country's first "shopping carts" among its products. Coller noted the efforts of the Chamber of Commerce and the Area Development Corporation to attract new firms. Efforts to broaden the city's economic base dated back to the earliest years but seemed particularly important in the changing climate of the 1950s.

The federal government continued to operate the Veterans Hospital complex and converted Percy Jones Hospital into the Federal Building in 1954. A major civil defense program headquartered there, as did the Defense Logistics Services Center, which installed the world's largest on-line logistics data bank in the 1970s. But the government also closed Fort Custer in 1968, leaving behind a ghost town and a hole in the local economy. The city made a dramatic bid to turn the abandoned land to positive use, purchasing the first 1,800 acres from the government in 1969 for an industrial park.

With the help of the Chamber of Commerce and Battle Creek Unlimited, the Industrial Park became a reality—the largest Class A park in the state. Mayor Frederick Brydges worked tirelessly to attract new firms to the park, where

land prices varied according to the number of new jobs that a prospective customer might generate. Keiper, USA, and a Japanese firm, T.S.K., arrived in 1978. Battle Creek became a Customs Port of Entry and a Foreign-Trade Zone as well. Soon new plants, both foreign and domestic, brought brightly colored buildings and new hope to the area.

Downtown Battle Creek was not to be left behind. In 1974 the city turned congested Michigan Avenue into a pedestrian mall with peripheral parking to encourage shoppers. Refurbishing of old buildings continued, and the Downtown Merchants' Association promoted a variety of activities to bring people back.

Stouffer's Hotel symbolized renewed enthusiasm for the downtown area in 1981. Visitors to the luxurious "McCamly's Roof" restaurant look out upon a scene far different from the pioneer world of a century and a half earlier. The hills were there when Sands McCamly first came in 1831, but he could never have imagined the changes 150 years would bring. Modern viewers can read the history of the town in the scene below. The outlines are still visible of the canal that brought waterpower to McCamly's first industries. The streets follow roughly the outline he and his associate platted. But the buildings tell of other chapters in the town's history. The first wooden storefronts were disappearing by the end of the Civil War, and the oldest buildings chiefly date from the boom years that followed. Red brick and local sandstone mark the older buildings, as does the white-painted wood of an occasional survivor from earlier years. Newer and taller buildings marked the turn of the century, like the seven-story Post Building at McCamly and Michigan.

In the 20th century land was expensive and hopes high. Steel and concrete made "skyscrapers" possible, and the towers of the Twenties remind us of those exciting years. Newer structures like the Michigan Gas Company and the American Bank Building ushered the city into the "modern" era after World War II; the new Transportation Center on the consolidated rail line marks present thinking. Most exciting for the future of the downtown may well be the construction of the new Kellogg Company headquarters on McCamly Street.

The city's heritage and its strength show through in its buildings and in its people. Sands McCamly helped the community through its infant years. Edwin Nichols, A.C. Hamblin, Loyal Kellogg, and others moved it into prominence as a 19th-century factory town. They built their great houses along Capital Avenue north of the creek. C.W. Post left his mark at the turn of the century, as Will Kellogg did later. Oak Hill Cemetery lies southeast on a rise of ground near the river. The McCamlys and Merritts, the Tituses and Hamblins, the Posts and the Kelloggs are there, along with Sojourner Truth.

But Battle Creek is more than its great buildings and famous people. The men and women who worked in the factories and tended shop left their mark as well. Their homes line the streets. Their children went to school. Their sons and daughters left for war. They paid their taxes and voted on the issues. They helped set the future course of Battle Creek in 1982, when they chose to accept the merger plan joining the city and the township and boosting population overnight from 35,000 to 56,000.

To the south of the Stouffer tower lies the new Lakeview Square shopping mall. To the east, Kellogg and Post plants. To the north the college and Leila Hospital. To the west the Federal Building, the airport, and the industrial park. Everywhere are signs of the city's past, and of its future. In Leila Arboretum stands a 22-by-28-foot cabin built of cherry and beech logs hewn to the mark. Scores of volunteers dismantled this ancient homestead, numbered the logs, and reassembled them next to the Kingman Museum in 1981 as a tribute to pioneer beginnings. A few weeks later the town celebrated the present with colorful pageantry as 23 countries sent representatives to the Fifth World Hot Air Balloon Championship.

Nineteen eighty-one was "A Year to Remember"—the theme of the sesquicentennial. As the chairman of the Albert L. and Louise B. Miller Foundation, Robert Miller, put it, the city must "recognize what we have" but remember that the past "is just the beginning." Perhaps the outdoor sculpture at the Transportation Center says it best; it's titled *Circa: Gateway to the Future.*

The city's first "skyscraper," the 1900 Post Building, is reflected in one of the downtown's newest buildings, the modern American Bank on McCamly Street. Courtesy, Peter J. Schmitt

95

CHAPTER VII
Partners in Progress

The annals of Battle Creek's industrial and business development comprise a fascinating story of geographical selection, entrepreneurial daring, a dependable labor force, and ingenious inventions. This heritage renders the city's history a colorful example of America at its best.

The pioneer settlement of the 1830s evolved into a depot for distribution of Calhoun County's agricultural production when the Michigan Central Railroad linked Battle Creek with Eastern-markets in 1845. Later entrepreneurs catering to local agricultural needs developed factories to produce a variety of farm tools.

The arrival of the Seventh-Day Adventist Church in 1885 provided the stimulus for the city's other fascinating 19th-century industries. The Adventist press blossomed into the largest operation of its type in Michigan, and literature bearing the Battle Creek imprint spread the city's name worldwide. The church's concern over rational health reform produced the Battle Creek Sanitarium which, under the flamboyant leadership of Dr. John Harvey Kellogg, became a mecca for the run-down rich and famous.

Dr. Kellogg's experimentation with health foods resulted in his invention of flaked breakfast cereals. The imaginative advertising of C.W. Post and W.K. Kellogg revolutionized America's eating habits and brought Battle Creek fame as the Cereal City. Kellogg's, Post, and the descendant of the Sanitarium, the Adventist Hospital, remain very much a vital part of present-day Battle Creek.

But the city's history also demonstrates industrial and business evolution. As some 19th-century enterprises fell by the wayside, others born in the 20th century took their place. Albert L. Miller journeyed from Kansas in 1911 to turn a dying newspaper into what under three generations of Miller leadership has become a journalistic dynasty. The Clark Equipment Company of Niles constructed a plant to manufacture axles in Battle Creek in 1920 that has become a major producer of the firm's well-known forklift trucks.

In 1941 Howard J. Stoddard consolidated Battle Creek's City Bank and five other Michigan banks into the Michigan National Bank chain and brought renewed vitality to the area's financial system. That same year Harold and Ruth Swanson began a little enterprise on Upton Street that today stands as America's largest producer of home-style cookies—Archway. A group of local doctors, following the precepts of Dr. Andrew Taylor Still, banded together in 1945 to create the Lakeview General Osteopathic Hospital to offer citizens the alternative of osteopathic medicine.

The 1950s witnessed continued entrepreneurial success stories. John ter Avest emigrated from the Netherlands to build a reputable insurance agency. James R.C. Hazel came from the coal-mining area of Kentucky to launch his Marathon Oil Gas Station. His son, James R.C. Hazel II, followed his example to build his own Union 76 station into a national award-winning enterprise.

During the 1980s Battle Creek's reputation as a good place to do business drew such diverse new operations as Felpaush Food Stores from Hastings, Nippondenso Sales from Japan, Stouffer's Battle Creek Hotel, and the Lakeview Square Association. The following chapter relates the heritage of a variety of businesses that are proud to call Battle Creek home, and by so doing ensure the area's continued vitality.

Facing page: The Battle Creek Journal *carried this drawing of the L.W. Robinson department store in 1901. It showed the spacious interior appointments of Charles W. Post's lavish new skyscraper. Courtesy, Western Michigan University Archives*

BATTLE CREEK AREA CHAMBER OF COMMERCE

The Battle Creek Area Chamber of Commerce slogan, "We Mean Business," goes far beyond "making a living." The Chamber works to promote "a clean environment, quality educational opportunities, strong government . . . and a friendly city with progressive ideas." Nearly a thousand business and individual members may serve on a score of committees and projects to make greater Battle Creek "greater."

For more than 100 years area businessmen have fostered just such goals. As early as 1872 leading citizens formed the Manufacturers' Association, led by men such as banker Alex Hamblin, merchant T.B. Skinner, and miller Thomas Hart. A century ago the Businessmen's Association of Battle Creek vowed to "advertise the city abroad and do all they can to encourage immigration to our city, and in all ways help 'boom' the town." This group affiliated with the State Businessmen's Association in 1887. In August 1912 the

Two world hot-air balloon championships and the first North American hot-air balloon championship have been secured by the Battle Creek Area Chamber of Commerce.

old Industrial Association reorganized and became the Chamber of Commerce. Headquartered first in the Industrial Room of the Post Building, members took on projects of lasting significance. In 1917, for example, the Chamber played a major role in bringing Camp Custer to the area. During the Depression the group worked hard to attract new businesses. After World War II the Chamber bought and maintained a 100-unit veterans' housing project near Kellogg Field.

In 1960 the Battle Creek Area Development Board and the Better Business Bureau merged with the Chamber, which changed its name to the Battle Creek Area Chamber of Commerce. Kermit Krum then pledged a "common goal—building a greater Battle Creek." By 1970 the Chamber was forming an Industrial Development Fund, promoting Fort Custer land development, and publishing *Livibility*, a magazine stressing "the greatest assets of living in Battle Creek."

Today the Chamber is the "front door" to Battle Creek, answering questions from individuals and

businesses alike, offering members a variety of research and statistical services. Current committees range from a "BAC-PAC" political action committee to the Visitor and Convention Bureau. Securing two world hot-air balloon championships and the first North American hot-air balloon championship ranks high among the Chamber's current achievements, as does formulating and carrying out the widely copied "Silent Observer" program to combat crime. The Chamber also houses the Visitor and Convention Bureau and Pride, Inc. Indeed, as one current brochure puts it, the "scope of Chamber activities is as broad as the needs of our community." Current Chamber board of directors chairman Jim Bell stresses, "We live in a rapidly changing world that requires tremendous adaptability on the part of individuals and organizations." The Chamber's Strategic Planning Committee monitors those changes, and its current Program of Work incorporates new policies and projects suited to a changing community.

Michael Jackson has headed the Chamber's seven-member professional staff since 1978. His office is decorated with brightly colored balloon posters and reminders of community projects such as a silver spike from the rail consolidation project. Tucked away among these mementos is one that says simply, "Expect a Miracle." As Jackson describes the world hot-air balloon championships, Fort Custer Industrial Park, or the projected linear park along the river, he gives the impression that the Chamber will continue to help make miracles happen.

LAKEVIEW GENERAL HOSPITAL/OSTEOPATHIC

The current facilities of the Lakeview General Hospital/Osteopathic include a $3-million addition, completed in 1974.

During the last quarter of the 19th century, Dr. Andrew Taylor Still founded a new medical discipline—osteopathy. Dr. Still developed osteopathy in reaction to the existing theories of homeopathy, allopathy, and eclecticism, which advocated treatment through massive doses of various drugs. Osteopathy favored treating not merely the disease, but the entire person including the social and physical environment. Furthermore, Dr. Still believed that a healthy body in skeletal and muscular balance and with proper circulatory and nervous functions could heal itself of many diseases. A unique contribution of this advanced discipline was the diagnosis and treatment of body malfunctions through the use of hands.

The more established medical disciplines fought fiercely against osteopathy, but the profession continued to grow. By the 1930s osteopathic medicine had become a major health care alternative which integrated the newest diagnostic and therapeutic techniques with its distinctive manipulative therapy, or biomechanics.

In 1944 fifteen osteopathic physicians in the Battle Creek area formed a hospital association. On August 26, 1945, their new hospital at 34 Elm Street stood ready for inspection by the community. The Battle Creek community, long a supporter of progressive medical theories, responded enthusiastically. Within a decade the hospital proved far too small to accommodate the growing number of patients.

In May 1955 over 400 citizens volunteered to join a public building fund campaign for a new hospital. Kenneth K. Parlin, general fund chairman, and Harold W. Herrick, chairman of the board of trustees, led a vigorous campaign. Individual pledges, private and corporate donations, and various fund-raising activities demonstrated generous public support. Major contributors included the W.K. Kellogg Foundation, the Kellogg Company, and Marjorie Merriweather Post.

On March 3, 1957, the trustees proudly dedicated the new Lakeview General Hospital/Osteopathic at 80 North 20th Street. The official open house in May hosted over 7,000 visitors who toured the modern, 56-bed, two-level, 29,780-square-foot facility. The hospital staff included 28 Doctors of Osteopathy. The board of trustees consisted of Harold W. Herrick, president; Walter L. Edgerton, first vice-president; Warren R. Speers, D.O., secretary; J.W. Meehan, D.O., treasurer; Hugh McPherson, second vice-president; Stanley K. Lassen; Kenneth K. Parlin; William Starkweather; Millard Vanderwoort; Robert N. Cobb; Keene W. Wolfe; and Clinton Stringham. Max W. Johns was the administrator.

The modern new facility, the only osteopathic hospital and osteopathic teaching hospital in southwest Michigan, soon needed additional space to meet the area's needs. In 1965 a new two-floor wing added 30 beds. In 1968 the completion of the second floor of the new wing gave the hospital a total of 112 beds. Then, in April 1974, a third expansion, a $3-million addition, opened. It increased the hospital's capacity to 167 beds including an 11-bed obstetrical suite, 32 beds for pediatrics and modern intensive care, and a cardiac and progressive care unit containing 12 beds.

Currently affiliated with Leila Hospital and Health Center, the Lakeview General Hospital/Osteopathic serves the Battle Creek community as a full-service hospital offering a complete and progressive range of both inpatient and outpatient treatment and care.

R.W. SNYDER COMPANY, INC.

Nearly every McDonald's orange drink east of the Mississippi and north of the Mason-Dixon line starts out in the R.W. Snyder Company in Battle Creek. One of the oldest firms in town, Snyder's produces crushed fruits, flavorings, and extracts for the food industry. Workers in the highly automated plant on Monroe Street specialize in "custom flavor creation" from apple to walnut, using everything from Michigan cherries to Mexican strawberries in 38 ice cream flavors and 19 toppings, as well as in slush and shake bases, soft-serve flavors, syrups, and extracts.

R.W. Snyder, founder.

Russell Snyder could scarcely have imagined today's fast-food outlets or the institutional market, but he did appreciate the ornate Victorian soda fountains so fashionable when he came to town in 1889. Snyder spent 15 years learning the flavor and extract business in Oswego, New York. Then he bought out R.S. Marsh's local bottling works and announced he would "manufacture all kinds of

pop and ginger ale next summer." Battle Creek was an exciting place in the 1890s. Hundreds of visitors came to the sanitarium. People talked of temperance movements and pure foods and extraordinary new products. C.W. Post and the Kelloggs experimented with packaged cereals and food drinks. Through it all, Russell Snyder bottled his pop and prepared his extracts, doing much of the work himself when labor was scarce. The city directory listed him year after year as a soft-drink and extract maker, until 1908 when he turned to flavorings and extracts alone.

Snyder was 63 when A.J. Bloomberg came to town in 1921. Five years later he and the younger man had become close friends. Business boomed, and the local papers announced that "Snyder extracts are known and sold from coast to coast." Snyder's son died suddenly that spring, however, and the older man invited Bloomberg to take over the enterprise. The two drew up articles of incorporation and asked Horace Mecham, Earl Kanaga, and Paul Ricketts to join them. Bloomberg headed the new corporation, and Snyder remained as vice-president until his death in 1940.

Bloomberg brought energy and new direction to the firm. In the early days Russell Snyder had tried his hand at Bay Rum, jeweler's lubricating oils, and medicinal preparations, but his flavors and extracts sold best. Wholesale druggists placed the biggest orders. They, along with candy and tobacco suppliers, distributed Snyder's products across the country. After World War II corner drugstores and small

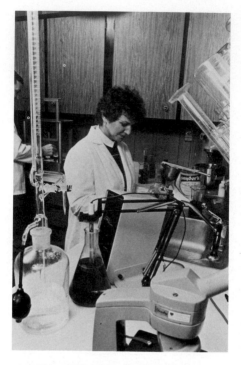

The firm's staff develops products with state-of-the-art equipment.

The R.W. Snyder Company, Inc., produces crushed fruit, flavorings, and extracts for the food industry.

candy shops declined, replaced by fast-food outlets and specialty stores. A.J. Bloomberg and his son sought to capitalize on this changing market. Over the years the R.W. Snyder Company gained an enviable reputation for its new bakery, dairy, and soda fountain products. In 1960, for example, when diet drinks caught the public fancy, the company developed "Dietal" and began producing the 900-calorie powdered food concentrate at the rate of 50,000 pounds a week.

The company moved to the simple brick building on Monroe Street in 1943. Battle Creek's mill race used to run past the front door, carrying water power for the town's pioneer industries. The canal has long since disappeared and primitive manufacturing with it. Battle Creek residents who remember summer jobs at Snyder's when they were growing up would scarcely recognize the operation today. Thirty people do the work of twice that number a few years ago. State-of-the-art computers control the mixing of tons of material down to the hundredth part of a pound. Formulas are mixed and cooked, cooled and packaged automatically and carried on to be labeled and loaded onto shiny trailer

This building has housed the firm's home office and manufacturing plant since 1943.

trucks for delivery elsewhere.

Computers control inventory, orders, formulas, and invoices, but R.W. Snyder is people as well. Jason Bloomberg now heads the or-

This vacuum cooker is used to make fancy-type fruits.

ganization and carries on traditions begun nearly a century ago. A modern research laboratory monitors quality and analyzes customers' needs. Sophisticated equipment helps technicians develop specialized products to meet individual requirements, while a pilot plant tests new manufacturing techniques.

Over the years Snyder's pursued new flavors and new markets around the world. The firm opened a second plant in Boyertown, Pennsylvania, and added a third in Taiwan in 1984. The newest facility will produce syrups and toppings for the Asian market, and manufacture mayonnaise, sauces, ketchup, and other condiments. The R.W. Snyder Company, Inc., approaches its 100th anniversary in a world its founder could not have anticipated; but as long as people order sundaes, slushes, and milkshakes, Snyder's will provide "combinations of flavors from around the world," for now the most exotic has become, with today's technology, the commonplace.

These steam-jacketed kettles are used to make a variety of syrups and toppings.

W.K. KELLOGG FOUNDATION

W.K. Kellogg's intention was clear at the outset when he established the philanthropic organization in 1930 that bears his name. His Foundation would "help people to help themselves." The man who pioneered the ready-to-eat cereal company in 1906 never wavered from his ideals during the years until his death in 1951 at the age of 91.

Since its inception, the W.K. Kellogg Foundation has distributed more than $767 million to pilot efforts in agriculture, education, and health. It currently funds programs in the United States, Latin America, and the Caribbean, as well as international fellowship programs in other countries. Few communities worldwide, however, have benefited so directly, and so measurably, from one man's business and philanthropic legacy as Battle Creek, Michigan.

Through the Foundation, W.K. Kellogg's personal concern for what he called "my hometown" has translated into economic and social betterment for Battle Creek. Local Foundation grants over the past 55 years have totaled nearly $41 million. They have affected nearly every aspect of community life: quality of education and health care, development of recreational facilities, enhancement of artistic and cultural programs, expansion of services for the handicapped, and support of initiatives to create new jobs.

The Kellogg Foundation's commitment to Battle Creek began with the Michigan Community Health Project in the early 1930s. It was a pioneering effort that showed (in seven counties surrounding the Battle Creek area)

W.K. Kellogg, who made his fortune pioneering ready-to-eat cereal, established the W.K. Kellogg Foundation in Battle Creek to "help people to help themselves."

that the health, educational opportunities, and general standard of living for families could be improved. The work involved public health services, childhood medical screening and care, and an extensive program of school and library improvement.

Similar activities have continued since then. For example, the Ann J. Kellogg School, named after W.K.'s mother, was built in 1930 to serve as a national model for mainstreaming the education of handicapped children into the regular K-12 school system. In 1977 the school received $4.5 million from the Foundation to modernize its facilities.

In recent years, Kellogg Founda-

tion aid has been directed at programs to provide in-service training for teachers and administrators, to boost learning for gifted and talented children, and to help young people become computer-literate. Kellogg Community College has received more than $9 million from the Foundation to increase its facilities and programs.

The Foundation has funded programs to expand the Battle Creek Child Guidance and Adult Clinic and the Family Y Center, to construct a high school learning center, and to provide a variety of employment opportunities for teenagers.

The quality of life of the community has been raised in many other ways. Funds were given for a public auditorium and a civic center/arena. Recently, nearly $1.5 million went to the Binder Park Zoo to expand its facilities and educational activities, and more than $3 million was awarded to the City of Battle Creek for a 28-mile linear park system.

Area hospitals, libraries, and other human service agencies have been aided by the Foundation in their efforts to improve the health and well-being of local citizens. A geriatric day–care program for the frail elderly and a hospice program for the terminally ill are local recipients of Kellogg Foundation aid.

The Foundation during the 1980s expects to direct a significant portion of its funds to other special initiatives to serve people in Battle Creek and Michigan. Such program support relates to current Foundation priorities in its three fields of interest. But attention focuses on economic development and youth-related efforts.

MICHIGAN NATIONAL BANK

The roots of the Battle Creek office of the Michigan National Bank extend back to 1871, when Nelson Eldred first opened the doors of the City Bank. In 1915 Cereal City citizens craned their necks to watch the completion of the eight-story skyscraper at the corner of West Michigan and Capital Avenue, which became the City Bank's new home and still remains headquarters for the Michigan National Bank in Battle Creek. The City Bank prospered through the following two decades, and when the Great Depression forced hundreds of Michigan banks to close during the 1930s, Battle Creek's City Bank remained solvent.

The Great Depression and the banking crisis of the early 1930s lured an ambitious young Mormon named Howard J. Stoddard from

the family lumbering business back into his early love, banking. In 1932 he joined the Reconstruction Finance Corporation, established by President Hoover to assist banks through the crisis. Few banks in the country were in deeper trouble than those in Detroit, and in 1933 Stoddard arrived in the Motor City to help unsnarl the financial mess. His work there and in other Michigan communities brought him a reputation as a master banker. By the end of the decade he had conceived the plan of organizing a banking chain to combine big-bank loan capabilities with small-bank consumer orientation.

Six key banks in major out-state industrial cities—Battle Creek, Grand Rapids, Lansing, Marshall, Port Huron, and Saginaw—were acquired, and Michigan National Bank opened for business on January 2, 1941.

Stoddard strongly believed that local autonomy was necessary to effectively serve each community. Local advisory boards, composed of business and community leaders, were established in each Michigan National city to assist the senior vice-president in charge. Glenn O. Hoffhines headed the Battle Creek office from 1941 to 1962, followed by Arnold Van Zanten from 1962 to 1977, Hugh M. Wright in 1978, Arnold J. Middeldorf from 1978 to 1982, and Richard H. Jones from 1982 to present.

The Central National Bank in Battle Creek was acquired in 1947 and merged into the Battle Creek office of Michigan National Bank. In 1953 the West End branch opened its doors as one of the most modern facilities of its type. It was Battle Creek's pioneer drive-in

bank, with four windows at which customers could "bank from the comfort of their cars."

"Banking that is building Michigan" has always been Michigan National's slogan. The institution pioneered push-out-type drive-in tellers' windows, Saturday banking, mobile home financing, and Michigan's first statewide credit card, Michigan Bankard. In 1972 Michigan National Corporation was formed. Rapid growth has ensued, and the holding company is now comprised of 26 banks with $6.6 billion in total assets, serving over 2.6 million customers in more than 200 Michigan communities through 353 banking offices and 750 automatic teller machines.

Howard J. Stoddard, founder of Michigan National Bank.

The Battle Creek National Bank (shown here under construction in 1915) became the headquarters for the Battle Creek office of Michigan National Bank in 1941.

KELLOGG COMPANY

It was 1894 and Victorian house-wives rose early to fire up massive wood-burning ranges and fry huge, greasy breakfasts. Dyspepsia was an everyday word. Dr. John Harvey Kellogg, superintendent of the Battle Creek Sanitarium, offered relief through a regimen of vegetarian diet, massage, and the water cure. He constantly experimented to develop health foods more palatable to his patients. That year he turned wheat grains into the world's first flaked breakfast cereal. The doctor's brother, Will Keith Kellogg, assisted him in this discovery but shared little of the glory. However, W.K. Kellogg, as astute and imaginative in his own right as his older brother, would be the one to revolutionize American breakfasts. He changed the image of flaked cereal from that of a health food to that of a quick and tasty alternative to heavy meals, and he indirectly freed American housewives from hours of daily toil.

W.K. Kellogg, age 46, about the time he founded Battle Creek Toasted Corn Flake Company. © 1983 Kellogg Company.

Both the Kellogg brothers cherished a belief that grains were the key to good nutrition. Throughout the 1890s they continued to experiment with various grains and processes. Their Sanitas Nut Food Company marketed caramel cereal, granola, and Granose Flakes Biscuits, and in 1898 they added cornflakes. These first cornflakes, made from whole corn kernels, were hard on the teeth, not too tasty, and grew moldy on the shelf. But when the Kelloggs turned to grits, The Sweet Heart of the Corn®, and W.K. added malt and sugar for better flavor, they had found the right formula.

Battle Creek remembers the early years of the 20th century as the "cereal boom." Entrepreneurs jumped at the chance to profit from this new American dietary fad. Over 40 strange-sounding products including Malta-Vita, Egg-o see, Try-a-bita, Per-Fo, Flak-Ota, and Cereola competed with the Kellogg's® Sanitas Corn Flakes. Most were quick to come and quick to go. The Kelloggs had an excellent product, but the doctor still considered it a medicinal remedy and prohibited aggressive advertising. W.K. Kellogg watched others make fortunes from cereal while his company plodded along.

By 1906, as he neared his 46th birthday, W.K. Kellogg knew what he must do. He launched the Battle Creek Toasted Corn Flake Company in a rickety old plant on Bartlett Street. Kellogg knew his product was good and believed that if consumers would once sample Kellogg's Corn Flakes® they would buy more. He also had a flair for innovative advertising. That first year Kellogg spent one-third of his

W.K. Kellogg, always fascinated by the plant operation, frequently inspected the Battle Creek facility. Photo circa 1930. © 1983 Kellogg Company.

working capital on a full-page ad in *Ladies' Home Journal* and gave away four million sample boxes, each labeled "The original bears this signature—W.K. Kellogg." Production swelled from 33 to 2,900 cases per day.

But Kellogg received a severe setback on July 4, 1907, when the plant on Barlett Street burned to the ground. Undaunted, Kellogg purchased a new site within the week. By January 1908 trainloads of Kellogg's Toasted Corn Flakes® chugged away from the new plant on Porter Street. In May 1909 the flourishing enterprise became the Kellogg Toasted Corn Flake Company. That year the firm sold over one million cases.

The company was a pioneer in the use of color in magazine ads, and by 1911 the advertising budget reached one million dollars per year. Innovations in manufacturing and packaging kept pace as well. The flavor and freshness of corn flakes improved dramatically in 1914 when Kellogg's replaced the traditional outer wrapper with a patented Waxtite® package liner. The firm also augmented its repertoire with Wheat Flakes in 1912, Kellogg's® Flaked Bran in 1915, and All-Bran® cereal in 1916.

During World War I American doughboys carried Kellogg's cereals to European battle fronts, and during the 1920s the company began exporting throughout the world. The firm launched its first foreign production plants in 1924 at London, Ontario, Canada; and Sydney, Australia. The famous Kellogg's Home Economics Department began developing new recipes and assisting consumers with nutrition information in 1923. The company first offered Rice Krispies® in 1928 as "a cereal so crisp it crackles in cream."

As hundreds of businesses floundered during the Depression years, far-sighted Kellogg doubled his advertising budget, and each year during the 1930s reached new highs in production and sales. Behind Kellogg's rather dour personality beat a heart of gold. During those bleak Depression days he shortened his plant shifts to create more jobs, put the unemployed to work constructing a 10-acre park, and established the W.K. Kellogg Foundation to "help people to help themselves."

The 1940s brought another world war and Kellogg Company did its part by packaging "K-rations" and continuing to develop nutritious breakfast foods including Kellogg's® Raisin Bran in 1942. The war years also marked the beginning of cereal fortification as Kellogg's voluntarily began adding nutrients to replace those lost in the milling process.

W.K. Kellogg died in 1951 at the age of 91, but the company he founded thrived during the first decade of the television era. Howdy Doody, Wild Bill Hickock, Superman, and Captain Kangaroo helped introduce that generation's children to Kellogg's® new ready-sweetened cereals such as Corn Pops®, Kellogg's Frosted Flakes®, and Honey Smacks®.

During the 1960s Kellogg Company began a major worldwide expansion program. The organization also diversified with the acquisition of Salada Foods Ltd. By the mid-1960s annual sales averaged 490 million pounds. Kellogg responded to consumer health concerns of the 1970s by increasing its cereal fortification and ingredient labeling practices. The acquisition of Fearn International in 1970 and a merger with Mrs. Smith's Pie Company in 1976 brought further diversification

The original Kellogg's Toasted Corn Flakes plant on Bartlett Street. Photo circa 1905. © 1983 Kellogg Company.

into the frozen-food market. By 1984 the firm employed over 18,000 people at 16 plants in 11 states and 22 foreign facilities.

In the 19th century the Kellogg brothers knew the importance of grain as a vital source of inexpensive nutrition. Kellogg Company remains a leader in developing, producing, and marketing grain-based foods. It recognizes that sophisticated technology is necessary to produce increased grain yields to feed an expanding world population. Kellogg Company has invested in Agrigenetics, a seed company performing research in genetic engineering, to be in the vanguard of this amazing new technology.

Throughout its colorful history, Kellogg of Battle Creek has become an American institution that influenced and adapted to cultural changes. Kellogg's grew up with the 20th century, and 20th-century America grew up with Kellogg.

Aerial view of the Kellogg Company headquarters—the world's largest cereal production plant. A new corporate headquarters building will be completed in downtown Battle Creek early in 1986. © 1983 Kellogg Company.

BATTLE CREEK GAS COMPANY

President William Thiel has been with the Battle Creek Gas Company for nearly 40 years. In all that time he has been most excited about the Lacey salt-cavern storage project in southern Barry County. Every day for a year, powerful pumps forced brine from a hole 3,000 feet underground, creating a cavern 130 feet in diameter and 120 feet high. One of the first salt-cavern storage facilities in the country designed for the storage of natural gas, it took six weeks to fill and held 125 million cubic feet of natural gas in 1973. With this first storage facility, Battle Creek Gas gambled and won. Local wells and storage gave a measure of independence from its pipeline supplier and guaranteed sufficient gas to industries locating in the new Fort Custer Industrial Park. As Thiel put it in 1978, future policy was clear: "We'd invest in the community's economic future."

Claude Wall, vice-president of operations at the time, played a very important role in the overall supervision of the Lacey Storage Field. Wall has been with the company for 34 years and is currently executive vice-president.

Battle Creek Gas has been serving the community ever since the first gas lights were illuminated at Clement Wakelee's store on Christmas Day in 1871. A group of bankers and businessmen had organized the firm in 1870. Headed first by Edwin C. Nichols, the fledgling enterprise included community leaders such as Victory Collier, Alonzo Noble, Nelson Eldred, Clement Wakelee, Thomas Hart, Richmond Kingman, and John Moulton, the first president.

At first, Battle Creek Gas con-
verted coal into illuminating gas and a "coke" by-product readily sold for heating and cooking. Battle Creek Gas installed 23 gas streetlights in early 1872, and a few years later paid $25 a month in wages for a lamplighter and his horse.

Battle Creek Gas grew slowly through the rest of the century, serving 600 customers in 1898, when David Henning offered $45,000 for the plant and properties. Henning, a wealthy Calhoun County investor with headquarters in Chicago, became president and W.A. Foote of Jackson, vice-president. Henning and Foote enlarged the company rapidly, adding hundreds of customers and putting up a new $12,000 office building at Michigan and Monroe in 1901. Henning died that same year and leadership passed to his son Edward, also of Chicago. Edward Henning sent David Henning Frazer to manage local operations and pushed the construction of giant metal storage tanks on Fountain Street. By 1914 Battle Creek Gas served 7,000 customers with 64 miles of mains. Another 4,000 subscribed over the next dozen years. Henning died in 1918, and
David Frazer, Jr., took over. During World War II Battle Creek Gas arranged with the Panhandle Eastern Pipe Line Company to provide natural gas for the first time. Under David Frazer, Jr., the organization continued to modernize its equipment and expand its service.

In the postwar boom years all customers were converted to natural gas; demand continued at such a rate that new customers took their places on a waiting list every year until 1960, when they totaled 20,730.

When David Frazer, Jr., died in 1964, David Eckman was elected president. Eckman had joined Battle Creek Gas in 1941 as general superintendent. He held the new post until 1975 and presided over one of the most challenging periods in American history. The energy crisis and skyrocketing inflation struck in the midst of prosperity. The firm's pipeline supplier repeatedly reduced available supplies. Industrial customers grew increasingly concerned.

Eckman led the company during

Battle Creek Gas Company's general accounting office and personnel during the Roaring '20s. Note the office was entirely illuminated by gas lights.

these critical years to explore vast storage facilities and local gas sources. A salt formation north of Battle Creek was thought to provide that storage capacity. In 1972 work began on the first of two underground caverns. Battle Creek Gas developed a closed system for washing away the salt. An eight-inch well sunk 300 feet into water-bearing sands provided 100 gallons of water a minute through a four-inch pipe drilled 3,000 feet below the surface. The resulting brine could be forced to the surface and, except for some drawn off by Barry County road crews, pumped over 6,000 feet back underground to a

sandy disposal zone. Within two years the firm had two such caverns in operation and the old metal tanks on Fountain Street could be dismantled.

In 1974 Battle Creek Gas signed an agreement with a competitor, Michigan Consolidated Gas, to buy all the natural gas in the newly discovered north-central Calhoun County field. That same year the company laid 17 miles of pipeline in 35 days to link the new "Cal-Lee" field to its Lacey storage area and to Battle Creek. Local gas began flowing through the pipes in January 1975. The storage cavern proved its worth in April when

temperatures fell 50 percent below normal. Battle Creek Gas weathered the second-coldest April on record without a single interruption to industrial users.

That same year saw a local oil and gas boom. Some 85 wells were sunk in the county—the third-highest total in the state that year. Battle Creek Gas also signed an agreement with Mobil Oil to purchase all gas discovered in a 216-mile area east of the city.

William Thiel became president in 1975, and these developments bore fruit over the next few years. By 1976 the company was pumping a million feet of gas a day from local sources, some 12 percent of all needs. By 1978 pipelines had tapped 36 wells and earnings topped a million dollars for the first time.

By the early 1980s Battle Creek Gas had completed over a century of service. It now counted 30,000 customers and took gas from 50 local wells. With the depleted Harris Well converted to storage, the firm could hold a billion cubic feet of gas in reserve and virtually guarantee its customers uninterrupted service.

The striking downtown headquarters of the Battle Creek Gas Company reflects the same faith in the community that Edwin Nichols and his partners displayed more than a century ago. Just as they and the Henning family later linked their fortunes with the town, so William Thiel and his associates look forward with confidence to the future in Battle Creek.

The underground storage well (foreground) and compressor station (background) of Lacey Storage Field.

Overall view of the firm's coke oven plant and storage holders. This manufactured-gas plant was the sole supplier of gas to Battle Creek until World War II.

Battle Creek Gas Company's new general office building on Michigan Mall was completed in 1965.

107

ARCHWAY COOKIES, INC.

In 1941 Harold and Ruth Swanson started a little enterprise on Upton Avenue to market their homemade baked goods. As they delivered their sweet rolls, fried cakes, and cookies to Battle Creek restaurants and groceries, one product stood out in particular—a large, moist, date-filled oatmeal cookie. Today the company they founded comprises the largest producer of "home-style" cookies in America.

When World War II produced a lack of shortening for frying, the Swanson Cookie Company turned exclusively to production of its specialty—home-style cookies of all descriptions. As the reputation of the Swansons' delicious cookies spread to other communities, they originated their distributor system to expand the market area throughout southern Michigan. One of the earliest distributors, Joe Bogdan, remembered selling an average of 5,500 packages to 260 outlets a week which he delivered in a half-ton panel truck. The cookies sold for 25 cents a package then, and gasoline cost 23 cents a gallon. Following World War II the Swansons added more distributors and new buildings and equipment to their Upton Avenue operation.

The year 1949 proved a milestone for the growing cookie company. George Markham, who would serve as president of the firm from 1963 to 1983, joined the organization. Also Leonard P. Ellis and his son, Donald, of Fort Wayne approached Harold Swanson with an offer to produce Swanson's Cookies in the state of Indiana. That was the beginning of a franchise licensing operation that brought the company international prominence. The Ellises provided

A view of Archway's corporate office, which is located in Fort Custer Industrial Park.

foresight and skill in assisting Swanson in developing a national network. During the next four years Swanson issued licensing agreements for the production and sale of cookies throughout the country.

The following year a trade name conflict with a frozen dinner manufacturer in Omaha, Nebraska, resulted in a new name for

The modern quality-assurance laboratory at Archway's corporate office.

Swanson's, Archway, derived from the original scalloped-arch logo on its package labels. Harold Swanson died tragically in 1954 following a heart operation that year and Ruth Swanson succeeded him as president.

The 1960s ushered in a new era of redirected goals and objectives. In 1963 George Markham became president of Archway Cookies, Inc. He formed a corporate national headquarters in Battle Creek to centralize internal services and organization. Archway grew dramatically during the '60s and '70s by emphasizing the effectiveness of the distributor system of product sales and quality control at every level of production. Becoming more marketing conscious, the company formed an in-house agency in 1975 to better coordinate overall marketing activities. Standardization of bakery uniformity, package labeling, and advertising became priorities.

A new headquarters building at 5451 West Dickman Road was completed in 1977. The structure houses the national corporate offices, marketing and advertising staff, data-processing center, and modern product-development, home-economist, and quality-assurance laboratories.

On March 26, 1983, after 20 years as president of Archway Cookies, Inc., George J. Markham retired. The company is now headed by Thomas F. Olin, chairman of the board, and Eugene H. McKay, Jr., president and treasurer. Archway owns two bakeries serving 38 states and maintains licensing agreements with six bakeries in the United States and one in Canada.

BATTLE CREEK SCHOOLS

W.K. Kellogg once said, "The greatest good for the greatest number can come only through education of the child, the parent, and the community in general." Throughout their 150-year history, Battle Creek Schools have consistently promoted just such a philosophy. Times have changed since pioneer children trudged to the first log cabin schoolhouse in 1834. Then one teacher taught every subject to every student; now the Battle Creek school system employs 1,200 people to meet the educational needs of the community. Ten thousand young people look to the schools to prepare them for the modern world. Today's school system includes the operation of two senior high schools, four junior high schools, one middle school, 16 elementary buildings, and an area vocational center. In addition, the school system operates the Willard Library, the W.K. Kellogg Auditorium, the Kingman Museum, and an Outdoor Education Center. The $90-million physical plant has been developed and maintained on a pay-as-you-go basis since 1950, and the school district has been completely debt-free since 1954.

Battle Creek Schools' education and outreach programs have roots as far back as the turn of the century, when educators realized that traditional teaching no longer met the needs of an urban and industrial society. Progressive educators opened the big, new Central High School building in 1909-1910. At the same time, the district introduced special education for students with learning disabilities and opened kindergartens for the very young. Battle Creek was one of the

The Willard Library (right) houses more than 155,000 volumes and an audiovisual center which contains an additional 25,000 films, tapes, and records. The library is owned and operated by the Battle Creek School District, whose administrative building is on the left.

first systems to introduce the new Parent-Teacher Association in 1913-1914. The Willard Library, opened in 1905 as part of the school system, brought with it the belief that learning was not confined to schoolrooms and ought to be available to the whole community.

Hard times struck America during the 1930s, but Battle Creek Schools expanded services. W.K. Kellogg once said, "I love to do things for children because I get a kick out of it." In 1930 he donated $245,000 to provide "mainstreaming" as a new opportunity for handicapped children. The Ann J. Kellogg School was one of the first in the nation to explore this concept when it opened in 1931.

During the 1930s the Battle Creek Schools developed a variety of programs to ensure that urban students had educational contact with the out-of-doors. The Kingman Museum of Natural History, opened in 1931 at the Leila Arboretum, then, as now, offers a variety of displays and programs to both students and community. The Outdoor Education Center, developed over the past 50 years on a 200-acre site 14 miles northwest of the city, operates programs in camping, gardening, pioneer homesteading, and farming.

In recent years the Battle Creek Schools have continued to introduce new services to the community. In 1956 the system opened a community college, which now enrolls over 3,000 students. In 1970 the school system began the operation of the Calhoun Area Vocational Center. A total of 25 diverse vocational courses are now available to secondary school students and adults from throughout the entire county.

A life-long resident, Mrs. Almon Jones, left a substantial gift to the schools in 1948 for "a community and social center." The Board of Education invested the gift and ultimately added a $.5-million grant from the Kellogg Foundation to build the Central High School McQuiston Learning Center in 1977. This elaborate 546-seat facility functions as a combined "community, civic, and social center" for a variety of activities. Perhaps no single edifice better illustrates the cooperation between schools and community than the W.K. Kellogg Auditorium. Given by Kellogg on his 65th birthday in 1933, this 2,000-seat auditorium serves as a cultural center, through the years attracting a host of big-name performers, bands, world-famous symphony orchestras, and ballet companies.

Pioneer schoolchildren could scarcely have imagined the complexity of the modern world; yet in every generation, the Battle Creek Schools have helped prepare the community for the world to come.

FEDERAL HOME COMPANIES

"What's in a name?" When that name is Federal Home Companies there's a story going back to 1906—a story involving the U.S. Congress and a special law signed by President Jimmy Carter, recognizing the importance of the name "Federal" when People's Home Life Insurance Company of Indiana and Federal Life and Casualty merged in 1977.

Both pre-merger companies began operations in 1906—People's in Frankfort, Indiana, and Federal in Detroit. Innovative policy writing and thoughtful mergers were keys to success then as now, and the new venture built solidly for the future. In 1953 Federal moved to Battle Creek under new ownership. Acquisitions and mergers continued on the parts of both companies. The Home Insurance Company, a large property-casualty insurer, bought both companies and the two joined forces in Battle Creek in 1969. In 1977 the two firms merged formally under the

Federal Home's corporate headquarters at 78 West Michigan Mall. In 1970 the firms moved their entire operations from the older building just beyond, and adjacent to, the present offices.

The present Federal Home's roots go back to Detroit and a company called Federal Life and Casualty. This building on West Grand Boulevard became home to that company when it was purchased by a Battle Creek group and moved to the Cereal City in 1953.

One of the amenities enjoyed by employees of the Federal Home Companies is the comfortable, attractive lounge which is enjoyed during noon hours and for employee activities. Adjacent to the lounge is a cafeteria serving healthful, inexpensive lunches each day.

Indiana charter of People's Home. Michigan congressmen secured special legislation authorizing the new company to continue the Federal name. The new merged company and its affiliate, PHF Life Insurance Company, became the Federal Home Companies.

With $6.5 billion of life insurance in force, the Federal Home Companies now rank in the top 12 percent of insurers nationwide, but still look for new programs. For example, the companies' "Enterprise Life policy" now offers a wide range of money-managing options for today's sophisticated customers. In 1946 Federal's 40th-anniversary publication promised clients "the same high quality of service and just treatment of past years, together with every possible benefit that constant research and striving may develop in the years to come." Insurance programs are far more elaborate today, and the number of policies in effect is so large that

the old standards of prompt and personal service would be impossible without modern technology. Green eyeshades and thick ledger books are gone—replaced by computers.

Federal has upgraded its equipment to keep pace with new developments, three times in the past 10 years, adding $.5 million in software in 1983 and another $.5 million in hardware in 1984. Agents now use hand-held computers for quick and accurate answers to questions in the field. Mainframe computer storage simplifies record keeping and frees the staff to deal personally with policyholders and their problems. With a little help from technology, insurance is still just as much "a people business" as it was in 1906—and today Federal Home can respond as quickly to thousands as its founders would have responded to hundreds of policyholders in the horse-and-buggy days.

JOHN TER AVEST AGENCY INC.

America was built by immigrants who traveled from distant shores to create new homes in a new nation. The story of Battle Creek insurance agent John ter Avest demonstrates that America continues to prosper as a recipient of immigrant dreams.

John ter Avest was born in 1922 in Nyverdal, Overijsel, in the Netherlands. After high school he went to work in a textile plant office. Then Hitler's lightning capture of the Netherlands in May 1940 changed life for all Hollanders. The textile plant closed and ter Avest secured a job in city hall, administering food ration stamps. Despite tight Nazi scrutiny he was able to surreptitiously dispense stamps to those who needed them the most. He also became active in the underground movement, and throughout the war he heroically assisted Jews escape Nazi jurisdiction.

When the Allied forces liberated Holland in 1945, ter Avest was appointed a detective in the police force because of his record in the underground. But police work did not appeal to him, so he left after a year and a half to launch a business that sold and repaired bakery machinery. ter Avest's wife, Gerry, had visited the United States following the war. They decided that they wanted to raise their family in a free country without the threat of war.

In December 1951 they arrived in the land of opportunity. Southwest Michigan was to be their new home. Their sponsor recommended Battle Creek as promising greater opportunity for the new arrivals since the other metropolitan areas, Kalamazoo and Grand Rapids, al-

ready had heavy Dutch populations. John Carton, a prominent Battle Creek insurance company president, gave ter Avest a job as a maintenance man in the Wolverine Tower. In October 1952 he began selling insurance, and in July 1953 John Carton hired ter Avest as a general agent for the Federal Life and Casualty Company.

Over the succeeding years, John ter Avest's hard work, personal charisma, desire to prove that he was a good American, and the fact that he represented a particularly reputable insurance company brought success. In 1956 he landed his biggest sale when the government of Holland bought insurance for 17,500 refugees. Gerry ter Avest, a deacon in her church, also assisted her husband through her community involvement. In the 1950s she began a local tradi-

tion by delivering Thanksgiving and Christmas dinners to needy persons. Barbara Downs joined the firm as secretary in 1959, and her outstanding service, particularly to older people fighting their way through Medicare red tape, spurred a growing word-of-mouth reputation.

John ter Avest also became very active in community affairs. As a trustee and president in the Presbyterian Church, treasurer and president of the school board from 1967 to 1980, and member of the board of the Child Guidance Clinic from 1967 to 1969, he gave generously of his time. In 1975 ter Avest became the area's first naturalized citizen to serve on the Calhoun County Selective Service Board.

Honors flowed to ter Avest. In 1968 he received the Daughters of the American Revolution Americanism Award for "trustworthiness, service, leadership, and patriotism." In 1972 the Battle Creek Jaycees named ter Avest the Boss of the Year. A special honor came from his son Simon in 1975 when he chose to follow in his father's footsteps and join the agency. John's other son, Jerry, currently a student, has also assisted in the growth of the agency.

John ter Avest has worked hard since he landed in America in 1951 and has built a career that is a credit to his new country. Perhaps his ultimate success can be measured by a statement made by a local attorney, Daniel Jaquint: "It is an honor to have John ter Avest as an insurance agent—and as a friend."

John ter Avest (seated), founder, with his sons, Jerry (left) and Simon.

ISRINGHAUSEN, INC.

"Isringhausen" might not be a household word for most Americans, but long-haul truckers, farmers, and heavy-equipment operators are discovering that it spells comfort for people who spend hour after hour behind the wheel. Isringhausen keeps them in the driver's seat with specially designed seating systems for the transportation industry. Founded in Germany after World War I, Isringhausen now makes its seating systems in factories around the world.

When Battle Creek Unlimited invited the firm to consider the Fort Custer Industrial Park for its American headquarters, the company established Isringhausen, Inc., in 1980. The new manufacturing and distribution center at 5450 West Dickman Road joins other operations in Argentina, Brazil, England, and France, as well as in West Germany. The firm's ISRI® seat and springs meet exacting requirements for driver safety and comfort worldwide, and all parts are interchangeable wherever manufactured.

Ever since its early efforts to improve bicycle saddles, Isringhausen has worked to provide comfort and safety to people who make their living in their equipment. A successful seating system for a world market would have to adjust to drivers of all sizes and dampen vibration, the heavy-equipment operator's constant irritation. The ISRI® seat offers professional drivers very necessary advantages. Short or tall, heavy or slight, drivers can easily adjust the seat and seat back for personal comfort while in motion.

Road- and equipment-induced vibration contributes to fatigue and

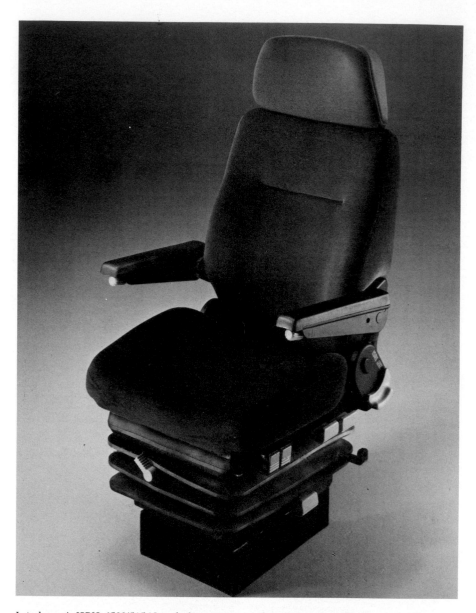

Isringhausen's ISRI® 6500/515AL is the latest version of the firm's air suspension seat with air lumbar support familiar to long-haul truckers, farmers, and heavy-equipment operators. The seat meets rigid requirements for driver safety and minimizes vibration.

to more serious health problems like spinal compression. The ISRI® automatic air suspension system functions to dampen vehicle vibration and maximize air suspension performance.

Battle Creek is geographically located within close proximity to the greatest vehicle-manufacturing area in North America. Designers have done much to make those vehicles safer and more efficient, but most have neglected the driver's seating system. Isringhausen engineers feel they have doubled the "window of safety" for professional drivers by offering maximum comfort and automatic vibration control. People who work a full day behind the wheel agree, and Isringhausen has found a place in the seating market.

BATTLE CREEK ADVENTIST HOSPITAL

Ellen G. White, early church leader of the Seventh-Day Adventist Church, developed a system of healthful living beginning in 1863 that emphasized a balanced diet, pure water, fresh air, sunlight, rest, exercise, abstinence from harmful products, preventive medicine, and mental and spiritual health. Over 120 years later the sensible principles she taught still comprise the basis of Adventist medical philosophy.

In 1866 the Church founded the Western Health Reform Institute in Battle Creek to offer hydrotherapy, dietary, and exercise treatments as an alternative to the era's often-deadly medical practices. A decade later newly graduated Dr. John Harvey Kellogg joined the institute as superintendent and launched an energetic building campaign. He constructed a massive new building and renamed the institute the Battle Creek Sanitarium. Under Dr. Kellogg's dynamic leadership the "San" became, by 1885, the "largest institution of its kind in the world."

Kellogg's life comprised an amazing epic of invention and scholarship. During his 91 years he wrote hundreds of articles and nearly 50 books with a circulation of over one million copies. He originated many health foods, including peanut butter, granola, and cornflakes, which indirectly launched the Battle Creek cereal industry. Kellogg also tinkered with mechanical devices to invent the universal dynamometer, a strength-testing device;

skin-tanning lights; and a mechanical exercise horse ridden by President Calvin Coolidge in the White House. A world-famous surgeon, Kellogg performed more than 22,000 specialized operations.

In 1902 the San burned, but Kellogg soon rebuilt an even more impressive facility. In 1928 he added a 15-story Central Towers Building, the tallest structure in the city. As the San gained worldwide fame for its therapeutic successes, thousands of run-down patients checked in annually. President William Howard Taft, Henry Ford, John D. Rockefeller, George Bernard Shaw, Dale Carnegie, Johnny Weissmuller, Thomas A. Edison, Eddie Cantor, and Amelia Earhart were some of the diverse celebrities who benefited from the San's regimen.

The Great Depression brought hard times for the San but it survived on a smaller scale. In 1942 Kellogg sold the huge main building to the U.S. government and it became the Percy Jones General Hospital. He moved his operation up the street to a beautiful fieldstone structure that he had purchased in 1913 for an annex. The facility had been constructed in 1899-1900 as the Phelps Medical and Surgical Sanitorium. The Phelps Sanitarium went bankrupt in 1904; C. W. Post acquired it and leased it to America's prototype strongman, Bernarr Macfadden, who operated another sanitarium briefly.

Following Dr. Kellogg's death in

1943, the Battle Creek Sanitarium continued to operate from the fieldstone building. In 1957 a group of Adventist doctors from California purchased the facility and in 1959 renamed it the Battle Creek Health Center. This name was used for about seven years, then in 1966 the sanitarium name was restored just before the centennial celebration. President Lyndon B. Johnson and Dr. Charles L. Hudson, president of the American Medical Association, arrived in Battle Creek to honor the century-old, Adventist-oriented institution.

The Battle Creek Sanitarium began a new era of development in 1970, when a modern, new $2.7-million hospital wing was dedicated. It was named in honor of Dr. James R. Jeffrey, who started at the San as a janitor in 1911. After Kellogg's death, Jeffrey acted as medical director for over 30 years. The sanitarium became an acute-care hospital in 1972 with medical, surgical, and mental-health facilities. In 1974 the Battle Creek Sanitarium Hospital, which had been the first Seventh-Day Adventist facility, again came under direct ownership and control of the church. It became number 394 of today's 470 SDA health-care institutions. The facility has now become a specialty hospital with primary emphasis on psychiatric care and alcohol/substance abuse treatment. In 1981 the name was again changed, becoming Battle Creek Adventist Hospital.

FELPAUSCH FOOD CENTERS

Hastings' Credit and Delivery Store, where Rome Feldpausch first started in 1928.

Felpausch Food Center's first Battle Creek outlet in Penfield Township.

Constantine Feldpausch's turn-of-the-century general store in Fowler, Michigan, stocked just about anything the community needed, from kerosene lamps and muskrat traps to open barrels of pickles and crackers. Farmers, venturing into town for their week's shopping, felt at home as they toasted their feet at the potbellied stove and swapped the latest stories. Times have changed, but the supermarket chain evolved by Feldpausch's descendants still practices the old-fashioned philosophy of making customers feel at home while offering them the best available food quality and values.

Feldpausch sold his general store and the meat market operated by his son, Gregory, in 1907 and purchased a pair of farms near Hastings. By 1911 Gregory had had enough of the vagaries of farming, and with five dollars in cash and an $800 note endorsed by his father he opened a butcher shop in Hastings. The following year Feldpausch went into partnership with his brother-in-law, Mike Fedewa. By 1922 their F&F Market offered a full line of meats, groceries, and produce. Grocery stores such as the F&F Market operated differently from today's self-serve supermarkets. Customers called in their order for home delivery or visited the store with a grocery list which clerks filled for them. Credit sales comprised two-thirds of F&F's volume.

Gregory's son, Rome, began working for his father after school and on Saturdays in 1917. Rome attended Notre Dame University from 1922 to 1926. He had an idea while going through the university cafeteria: Why not operate a self-serve grocery? In 1927 he was back working at F&F and the following year, when he purchased his uncle's interest, it became the Feldpausch Market—later the "d" was dropped to facilitate correct pronunciation. In 1933 the Feldpauschs converted the showroom of an old Pontiac garage into a novel concept—the Feldpausch Warehouse, where customers helped themselves and paid cash.

As the innovation caught on, expansion proved necessary. In 1940 they purchased the adjacent building which became the site of a 44- by 82-foot market—an enormous store for those days. Rome Feldpausch also purchased a farm in 1943 to raise beef and poultry for the market. Throughout the '40s and early '50s the Felpausch Food Market grew in size to satisfy customer demands. The year 1954 brought the first expansion into another community when the Felpausch Food Center in Albion opened. This operation proved successful and another Felpausch market opened in Eaton Rapids in 1956. From 1960 to 1978 Felpausch opened markets in Marshall, Mason, Grand Ledge, Coldwater, Williamston, Bellevue, Delton, Charlotte, and Leslie.

After studying the Battle Creek market area for over a decade, the Felpausch organization launched its first store there in 1980. The Penfield Township supermarket opened as one of the most unique stores in the Tri-State area. Two years of analyzing stores across the country resulted in an avant garde design with fully carpeted floors, sophisticated new equipment, and an in-store bakery intended to fill the distinct needs of the community. In 1982 Felpausch converted two former Hamdy and Kroger stores at North Avenue and the Columbia Plaza plus opened a new Food Center at the Urbandale Plaza.

Currently, the Felpausch organization operates 18 retail food stores and two lawn and garden centers throughout southern Michigan. Over 1,200 employees comprise the Felpausch "family," which works together for success.

NIPPONDENSO SALES, INC.

July 7, 1980, proved an auspicious day for Battle Creek's industrial future as citizens gathered for the opening of Nippondenso's new Battle Creek Distribution Center located in the heart of the new Industrial Park. Dignitaries from around the world who attended the dedication ceremonies that day included Takeaki Shirai, chairman, Nippondenso Company Ltd., Japan; Governor William Milliken; Congressman Howard Wolpe; State Senator Harry De Maso; and State Representative Richard Fitzpatrick. Akira Kataoka, president of Nippondenso Sales, Inc., and Donald Hensick, newly appointed Battle Creek operations manager, officiated at the festivities. The selection of Battle Creek as the site for this new enterprise was a coup that culminated a vigorous campaign by Battle Creek Unlimited as well as the support and assistance of Governor Milliken.

Nippondenso Company Ltd. of Japan had been established in 1949 as an offshoot of Toyota Motor Company Ltd. By 1984 it had become the world's largest manufacturer of motorcycle electrical components and one of the world's largest manufacturers of automotive electrical items. Nippondenso's more than 29,000 employees perform a worldwide network of manufacturing, sales, marketing, research, and product-development functions. Nippondenso Sales, Inc., is the company's United States sales and marketing unit.

Major U.S. automotive customers encouraged a rapidly developing business for the new Battle Creek facility. By its third year of operation Battle Creek, in conjunction with the Nippondenso

The Battle Creek Distribution Center of Nippondenso Sales, Inc., operates out of this facility at 400 Hill Brady Road.

sales facility, which had been in operation in Detroit since 1975, and the Service Center in Cedar Falls, Iowa, in operation since 1976, generated over $65 million in sales. The Battle Creek Distribution Center reinforced the automotive side of the business to consolidate distribution through a single central facility situated in the heart of automotive industry territory. Daily shipments of starters, alternators, fuel pumps, and other automotive engine, air conditioning, emission control, electronic, body, and safety related products routinely flowed to such destinations as Ypsilanti; Dearborn; Kansas City; Milwaukee; Oklahoma City; Edison, New Jersey; Lorain, Ohio; and London, Ontario, Canada.

The Battle Creek operation initially functioned with minimal staffing: Donald Hensick, operations

manager; Michael Maurer, warehouse manager; Peter Mortlock, traffic; and Laveta Kauffman, secretary. But when increasing sales volume and local content law implications called for new ventures, Nippondenso opened its second U.S. assembly plant in Battle Creek in October 1983. It was located in rented facilities in the Brydges Cargo Center and initially employed 40 personnel who assembled automotive heaters, blowers, and windshield washers. Future plans may include the construction of more permanent facilities to take advantage of Battle Creek's skilled labor pool.

The firm's Battle Creek Assembly Plant is located in the Brydges Cargo Center.

LAKEVIEW SQUARE

August 3, 1983, marked the beginning of "a new direction" in shopping for residents of south-central Michigan. A crowd of thousands arrived to view the magnificent new retail complex opened by Forbes/Cohen Properties—Lakeview Square Mall in Battle Creek.

The 650,000-square-foot, $40-million shopping mall is just one of Forbes/Cohen's large-scale developments. The Southfield, Michigan, firm began building and operating malls in 1967 and now owns the Lansing Mall, Westwood Mall in Jackson, and Maple Hill Mall in Kalamazoo, in addition to Lakeview Square. Two of the company's properties have since been expanded and it has added two office complexes in the Detroit area to its business portfolio. There are plans for additional developments in Michigan and other parts of the country as well.

However, for the partnership of Sidney Forbes and Maurice Cohen—and the entire Battle Creek community—Lakeview Square is a center of which they are all especially proud.

The Forbes/Cohen dream of a regional shopping center in Battle Creek began some seven years prior to the 1983 opening. As the firm conquered each construction challenge during those years, it grew more dedicated to making its newest mall the ultimate expression of quality and beauty. By the time construction was completed, the entire community was caught up in the excitement of having the latest in shopping right in its own backyard.

Opening-day shoppers, and the many who have visited Lakeview Square since, have seen the

Lakeview Square's modernistic advertising sign stands as a beacon to area shoppers.

Forbes/Cohen talent for combining the strictest of construction standards with pleasing artistic beauty while maintaining a concern for the environment. For example, it rerouted a state-designated trout stream that flowed through the construction site to enhance, rather than upset, the site's ecological balance. A landscape plan dotted with more than 20,000 plantings, many saved from the original site, transformed the formerly barren property into a park-like setting.

Inside the 112-store, one-level complex exists another landscape resembling a charming village street. Each design element—from the towering sculptures created by Michigan artists to the thousands of trees and flowering plants—reflects a warm, contemporary style.

In a climate-controlled, garden atmosphere, shoppers wander through a blend of national and locally owned shops anchored by Hudson's, Sears, and JCPenney. In contrast to Lakeview Square's contemporary mood, Picnic, the mall's Art Deco-style food court, might well remind diners of an earlier era famous for its flappers and jazz. Picnic has also made history by being the first such food court in Michigan outside the Detroit area. The individual food establishments surrounding the 300-seat central dining area offer a choice of ethnic and modern cuisine.

When the entire Lakeview Square development plan is complete, visitors to the commercial complex at the I-94 and M-66 cloverleaf on Battle Creek's south side will also enjoy, under a separate roof, the offerings of theaters and additional restaurants.

The overwhelming response to this bright new center of the '80s is proof that Lakeview Square is already part of the heritage of the "best-known city of its size in the world." And for Sidney Forbes and Maurice Cohen, the mall is their contribution to Battle Creek's new direction in growth: a contribution that is helping to expand the Cereal City's reputation as a place to stop for much more than just breakfast.

Lakeview Square's spacious center court combines the aesthetic with the functional.

STOUFFER HOTEL

When Mr. and Mrs. A.E. Stouffer opened a little stand-up dairy counter in downtown Cleveland in 1922 they little dreamed that six decades later the Stouffer Corporation would comprise a four-division operation with annual sales in excess of $.5 billion.

The imposing 15-story Stouffer Hotel, at 50 Capital Avenue Southwest, opened in November 1981.

The first modest expansion in this American success story came when Mahala Stouffer began sending her Dutch apple pies to the lunch counter. Her home-style recipes brought customers back, and in 1924 the first Stouffer restaurant opened in Cleveland—"The Stouffer Lunch." The Stouffers' son Vernon joined the business in 1924; he was followed by Gordon in 1929, the year the Stouffer Corporation was formed. The bleak Depression years and World War II temporarily interrupted expansion, but during the late 1930s and following World War II, new Stouffer restaurants opened in major downtown locations.

The 1950s brought expansion into the burgeoning suburban areas across the country. Also in 1954 Stouffer first entered the production and marketing of frozen prepared foods. By the 1980s Stouffer Foods had become the nation's leading producer of premium-quality, frozen prepared foods with more than 90 retail items.

The decade of the 1960s saw the acquisition of the first Stouffer Inn—the Anacapri at Fort Lauderdale, Florida. Soon other hotels and inns in Michigan, Illinois, Missouri, Ohio, Kentucky, Indiana, Pennsylvania, Georgia, Virginia, Colorado, Texas, and Arizona carried the Stouffer name as a beacon to travelers seeking quality and comfort in hospitality and dining. By 1984 Stouffer Hotels had grown into a national chain of 23 hotels. In March 1973 Nestle, S.A., headquartered in Vevey, Switzerland, acquired the three Stouffer divisions.

The concept of McCamly Square in downtown Battle Creek

Local investors, interested in urban renewal, pooled their resources to construct the $26-million McCamly Square on the area outlined in black.

grew out of the planning of an urban-renewal project group. Retired newspaper publisher Robert Miller headed a team of local investors who pooled their resources to begin construction of the approximately $26-million complex featuring a sports arena and exhibition hall (Kellogg Center), a retail shopping area housing two dozen specialty stores, and a hotel. Robert Miller wanted the best hotel facility between New York and Chicago so he selected Stouffer, famous for its family-type operation. Stouffer invested its professional skills into the project and in November 1981 the majestic 15-floor Stouffer Hotel opened.

The hotel's 248 rooms, including 15 luxury suites, a 600-seat ballroom, 2 restaurants, and an indoor pool, give Battle Creek its most luxurious hostelry since the glory days of the "San" and Post Tavern. Three meeting rooms, the Branson, Montgomery, and Custer rooms, with a total capacity of 840 in banquet or 1,270 in seating, provide for modern convention needs and have spurred an increase in business for the downtown area. McCamly's Roof, a 170-seat dining facility, and the adjacent City Lights lounge offer a view of the city comparable to that from a hot-air balloon ride. On the ground floor an English pub atmosphere offers more casual dining in J.W. Barleycorn's.

Stouffer Battle Creek Hotel became the 23rd in its nationwide chain. The corporation's interest in the continued revitalization of the downtown area demonstrates its commitment in participating as an active partner in the Cereal City's community development.

BATTLE CREEK ENQUIRER AND THE MILLER FOUNDATION

"We recognize ourselves as the appointed agent of the home, in honor and fidelity obligated to present a factual, honest, fair, and dependable record of the day's news." Albert L. Miller's words, spoken at the laying of the cornerstone of the new Battle Creek Enquirer Building in 1951, stand as a beacon to responsible journalism everywhere. More than eight decades of newspaper files document the *Battle Creek Enquirer*'s success in achieving those goals.

Albert Laird Miller, the youngest of seven children in a Kansas farm family, began newspaper work at the age of 12 as a printer's devil in Kansas. He learned the business in the heroic age of Kansas journalism when editors such as William Allen White and Henry J. Allen, once Miller's boss, commanded national respect. In 1907 Miller purchased the Ottawa, Kansas, *Herald*. That same year cereal magnate C.W. Post acquired the *Battle Creek Enquirer* which had been founded in 1900 by Joseph L. Cox, a printing press inventor and local politician. Post offered Miller the position of business manager in his newly acquired paper, but Miller found the plant in deplorable condition and declined.

By 1910 the *Enquirer* had been moved to better facilities at 7-11 McCamly Street, and Miller accepted Post's second offer. Before the year was over he took charge of the editorial department as well. In 1915 a larger building was erected on the McCamly Street site. In 1911 Miller established the *Evening News* as a counterpart to the *Morning Enquirer*, and in 1919 the consolidated *Enquirer and Evening News* became a six-day eve-

The office of the Battle Creek Enquirer *was located at 7-11 McCamly Street in 1910.*

ning and Sunday morning newspaper.

In 1928 Miller became president of the newly formed Federated Publications, Inc., which linked control of the *Enquirer and Evening News* with the Lansing *State Journal*, the Grand Rapids *Herald*, and later the *Journal and Courier* of Lafayette, Indiana. Miller served as president and then chairman of the board of Federated Publications until his death in 1958.

In 1953 Albert Miller's son, Robert B., became editor and publisher of the *Battle Creek Enquirer and Evening News* and president of Federated Publications. The firm continued to expand, adding papers in Indiana, Idaho, and Washington. In 1971 Federated Publications merged with the Gannett Company, Inc., and in 1979 Miller retired from the *Enquirer and Evening News*. His son, Robert B. Miller, Jr., the third generation of this journalistic dynasty, is now publisher of the *Battle Creek Enquirer*.

Following Albert Miller's death his widow, Louise Branson Miller, established a foundation in his

memory to "help things happen" in the community. Its first major contribution of $382,000 went toward construction of the Miller Physical Education facility at Kellogg Community College. The year 1983 marked 20 years of foundation activity with grants totaling $4,763,817, of which 90 percent were made within the greater Battle Creek area. The Albert L. and Louise B. Miller Foundation, dedicated to bettering the culture, economy, and quality of life in the community, has helped fund some 145 projects.

For over 70 years Miller family success in newspaper work has made Battle Creek a better-informed community, and since 1963 the Miller Foundation has returned some of the support that helped make that success possible by funding projects that make Battle Creek a better place to live.

The Battle Creek Enquirer Building, located at 155 West Van Buren Street, was completed in 1952.

A. RATTI AND SONS

Alex Ratti, Sr. (seated, center), immigrated from Italy to New York City in 1871. He relocated his family to Battle Creek in 1906 and opened the city's first ice cream parlor on West Michigan aided by (standing, left to right) his wife, Louisa, son Charles, and, beside their father (left to right), Alex Jr. and George. Alex Jr. is still active in the family's haberdashery business.

Some people think history is nothing more than names and dates they learned in school. Others find history all around them, everywhere. Alex Ratti, Jr., remembers turn-of-the-century Battle Creek as though it were yesterday. He's met people coming and going at 115 West Michigan since 1923 and helped out in his father's ice cream parlor long before that.

West Michigan is a quiet street today, quieter perhaps than it used to be. Sparrows still feed at the curbside and, while some of the buildings have a modern air, one storefront looks much as it did years ago. Red brick with white trim, it stretches 39 feet along the sidewalk—room enough for two

narrow shops and a staircase to the second floor. Above the second story, bold block letters read "Alex Ratti." A faded sign over 115 West Michigan announces "Men's Wear, Military." Alex Ratti constructed the building in 1913, and Alex Ratti, Jr., works there now, as he has for 61 years. Inside, the old display cases and tables are piled high with clothing, chiefly uniforms for fire, police, and postal workers. Blue walls and bright white enamel on the ornamental tin ceiling match rows of blue and white boxes on the wooden shelves.

Alex Ratti, Sr., left Italy and came to New York in December 1871, a 16-year-old alone, speaking no English, and with only a nickel in his pocket. A German immigrant family gave him a place to stay, and he learned quickly. Years later, he would help many other new immigrants himself. As a young man he traveled about the country, coming to Detroit as a

circus fortune-teller, but staying to become a candy maker. He prospered as a "confectioner," buying properties in Pontiac and Ann Arbor, marrying, and starting a family.

When his first wife died, he went back to Italy, where he married Louisa Sinelli. The couple returned to Ann Arbor to open a shop next to the University of Michigan. Alex Ratti, Jr., was born there in 1901. He remembers his first job in 1904, putting nuts on the candies his mother dipped in chocolate.

The Rattis came to Battle Creek in 1906, lured by a brother's praise of "the booming little town with the big industries." They rented 95 West Michigan from the Post family and opened the town's first ice cream parlor. High on the shelves today stands an age-darkened silver service with an elaborate centerpiece once used in the shop, as was a marble-topped table at the rear of the store.

After the ice cream parlor burned in 1923, Alex Ratti, Sr., and his sons opened a haberdashery at 115 West Michigan, selling men's hats for every season. When Alex Sr. died in 1927, George and Alex Jr. carried on. They turned to men's clothing as hats went out of style, and added military items during World War II. George died in 1968, and Alex remains, surrounded by old photographs and mementos of another era—a World War I helmet, early radios, trophies—and memories. The oldest businessman on the street, he is still very active today. "I could tell so many stories," he says, "if I only had time to sit down."

MASSACHUSETTS MUTUAL LIFE INSURANCE COMPANY

When Massachusetts Mutual Life Insurance Company opened its doors in 1851, most Americans were farmers, shopkeepers, or small businessmen. For a few cents a week, early insurance companies guaranteed policyholders a decent burial and little else. Times have changed; so has life insurance.

Mass Mutual is one of Battle Creek's oldest insurance firms, and its history mirrors those changes. The agency's founder, Charlie Jones, opened his office in 1917. The company gave him a territory covering 13 counties in southwestern Michigan. By 1943, when John Bromley joined as a co-partner, Jones' firm had weathered a quarter-century. Jones retired in 1949 after 32 years with Mass Mutual and Bromley replaced him as general agent.

With government and employers taking on more active roles in financial planning, the insurance business grew ever more complex. People no longer needed to die to reap the benefits of insurance plans. Mass Mutual helps supplement disability or retirement income and provide for college expenses or liquid assets with individually tailored programs. Bromley and his staff began to join with investment counselors, lawyers, and tax accountants to draw up elaborate money-managing packages for special clients. The agency specializes in pension, profit-sharing, and employee-benefit programs, particularly for small and medium-size businesses, and services over 400

such programs at present.

Bromley's successful recruiting of staff and innovative programs kept the agency consistently in the top 20 percent of Mass Mutual's national sales charts, and led to a close-knit organization with one of the lowest turnover rates in the country.

Peter Christ joined the agency in 1961 and was named general agent in 1970, when Bromley stepped down. John Bromley became one of 24 Mass Mutual agents with $100 million of policies in force in 1964. Ten years later Peter Christ had doubled that. The agency topped $400 million in 1983, with $80 million in sales.

But however complex insurance programs have become, human relationships still matter. When it comes time to file a claim, people often need advice as much as

money. Staff members read area newspapers each day, trying to anticipate clients in trouble. Often they reach clients before they have thought of filing claims. More than once the agency has helped families cope with death or disaster with answers to problems that seemed insurmountable. As a newspaper advertisement put it in 1966, "The one thing no other life insurance company can offer your family ... is a Mass Mutual agent."

Peter Christ left Battle Creek in 1984 to join Mass Mutual's home office as vice-president for pension services. But the traditions established by Charlie Jones and John Bromley and the direction set by Peter Christ are destined to continue. General agent Bromley's son, John R., now heads the agency as it approaches three-quarters of a century of service to the Battle Creek region.

General agents of the Battle Creek agency have included (from left to right) John R. Bromley, CLU, ChFC (1984-   ); John E. Bromley, CLU (1949-1970); and Peter J. Christ, CLU, (1970-1984). © J.M.T./john michael, Battle Creek.

JIM HAZEL'S UNION 76

During the early 1950s teen-aged James Hazel, Jr., began working at his father's gas station after school and on weekends. In those days huge gas-guzzling automobiles sporting fins on the back and massive grills on the front rolled up to the pumps to be filled up at 23 cents a gallon. Drivers routinely got their oil checked and windows washed. Those days are gone, but the traits of self-reliance, competitiveness, and perseverance that young Jim learned from his father continue as guideposts to his success.

James R.C. Hazel moved to Michigan from Kentucky in 1940. After a series of automobile-related jobs he left Battle Creek Auto Parts in 1952 to open a Marathon Oil gas station on Beadle Lake Road with $36 in working capital. Hazel acquired some farmland a mile south of his station which the newly built expressway, I-94, intersected during the late 1950s. In 1961 Hazel became one of the nation's pioneer U-Haul dealers.

When James Hazel, Jr., returned from studying engineering in college he saw an opportunity for a

The late James Hazel (right) with his son, James Jr., in 1968.

new station catering to expressway traffic. In 1964 Hazel opened a Pure Oil station on his father's land at 14301 Beadle Lake Road. The early years consisted of long hours of hard work as Hazel sought to build a prosperous business. From six in the morning until midnight, seven days a week, Hazel pumped gas and worked on cars. His dedication and personality paid off as he developed a loyal following. His father closed his station and joined him in a partnership until his death in 1978.

In 1968 the Hazels won national recognition for their efforts when the Pure Oil Company chose their business out of 16,000 other operators as Dealer of the Year. Hazel relied on his reputation for reliable service to further his business. The oil embargo of 1974 brought gas shortages and long lines at the

pumps, and changed many dealers' attitudes toward customers. But Hazel continued his old-fashioned philosophy of efficient, friendly service.

The third generation to be involved in the firm, James Hazel III, joined his father in a part-time capacity in 1981. Jim Hazel's Union 76 service station pumped an average of over 100,000 gallons a month in 1982 to win an award from the McLeier Oil Company as its largest-volume dealer. While many other stations have abandoned auto repair to become convenience store outlets, Hazel's station comprises one of the last full-service operations in the area to continue to offer mechanical repair services. Hazel employs 11 certified mechanics, operates an auto-parts store, and operates a repair service open from 6:30 a.m. to 10:00 p.m., seven days a week.

Hazel has become very involved in community affairs. He is active in the Harper Creek Optimist Club, one of the largest in the country, and became master secretary for the organization in 1979-1982. He belongs to the Masonic Lodge, Knights Templar, and the Battle Creek Small Business Council. Fund-raising drives for the Y Center, United Arts Council, and Binder Park Zoo have benefited from his dedication. Hazel also guides the Battle Creek Area Chamber of Commerce Leadership Academy, which prepares others for community leadership. He has been active in scouting since the age of 11. In 1980 the South West Michigan Boy Scout Council presented Hazel with its highest honor, the coveted Silver Beaver Award.

Two generations of Hazels, through long hours of hard work and a dedication to good service, created this modern Union 76 service station at 14301 Beadle Lake Road.

HI-LEX CORPORATION

Personal contacts mean a great deal in American business, and personal friendship brought Hi-Lex Corporation to the Fort Custer Industrial Park. Hi-Lex took its name from the control cables it makes for automotive and other uses. The story began in 1974, when Battle Creek Mayor Frederick Brydges made the first of many trips to Japan to meet with business leaders. There he saw Tomesaburo Teraura, founder of the giant Nippon Cable System which supplies 70 percent of all the mechanical cable controls for the Japanese auto industry. On each successive visit, Mayor Brydges met again with Teraura, and they came to like and respect each other.

Nippon Cable had been explor-

ing the international market for several years. In 1975 Teraura founded TSK of America, Inc., to manufacture cables locally. TSK's first client, the International Harvester Corporation, was followed shortly by Mercury Marine. "Come to Battle Creek," Mayor Brydges invited Teraura, offering "anything we can do for you in order to realize your dream." In 1977 ground-breaking ceremonies at the Industrial Park marked the beginning of one of the most automated production facilities in the United States. Nippon Cable invested $2.5 million in building and equip-

Mayor Frederick Brydges greets Tomesaburo Teraura, president of Nippon Cable System, during a visit to Battle Creek.

ment and followed with other support.

Edwin Matthewson was named president and chief executive officer in 1980. He presided over a name change from TSK to Hi-Lex and guided the business through the recession of the early 1980s. Despite an uncertain economy, Nippon Cable's president retained "great confidence for the future growth of the company." Hi-Lex increased its market each year, making striking gains in 1983, when the firm added 18,000 square feet to its manufacturing plant. A second 26,000-foot addition will be completed in 1984.

Hi-Lex presently manufactures mechanical control cables for automotive, marine, motorcycle, snow-

mobile, and many other industrial and farm-equipment applications. Though based in Michigan, Hi-Lex sends its products all over North America. Its customers are original-equipment manufacturers, notably in marine hardware, though automakers accounted for 25 percent of Hi-Lex sales in 1983.

Cable controls provide particularly innovative and cost-cutting improvements in the automotive field. Automakers have used Hi-Lex window, door, and brake cables, and the company also provides clutch, throttle, choke, and speedometer applications. In 1984 automotive cables may account for as much as 55 percent of the business.

Hi-Lex maintains its own engineering department to help customers design custom cable applications. Its main manufacturing plant contains a space-age array of heavy machines that turn

great drums of wire into coiled cable housing, automatically covered with flexible casing. Another machine prepares the cables' "inner member" and attaches end fittings. Electronic testing equipment provides quality control at several points along the assembly line. Cables operate in one chamber while temperatures change from negative 125 degrees Fahrenheit to plus 375 degrees. A salt-spray test monitors corrosion resistance. Tensile-strength testing, visual inspection, and dimension checks complete the quality-control cycle.

While Hi-Lex is an American company rooted in Battle Creek and serving a North American market, president Matthewson visits the parent corporation at least

---

Battle Creek's Mayor Frederick Brydges and To-mesaburo Teraura exchange gifts on the occasion of the mayor's visit to Japan.

twice a year. Not long ago, he planted a row of Japanese cherry trees in front of the plant as a tribute to Tomesaburo Teraura, who died in 1980. Hi-Lex' growth has been fostered by men like Teraura and Mayor Brydges, whose friendship transcended culture and language differences. Mayor Brydges once complimented Teraura on the strawberries in his garden. When word came that Brydges was very ill, Teraura "tried to let him eat Japanese strawberry again." His son, Makoto Teraura, picked a basket from the garden early one morning and flew to Battle Creek, where he brought the berries to Mayor Brydges' bedside that same day. Both men instrumental in bringing Hi-Lex to Battle Creek have died, but Nippon Cable's current president believes that "The true friendship between these two gentlemen will be continued by their respective successors forever."

CLARK EQUIPMENT COMPANY

"If each and every element of a company does its job well, the company prospers," wrote Eugene B. Clark shortly after he and a group of associates founded the forerunner of the Clark Equipment Company. More than eight decades of consistent growth have demonstrated the practicality of Clark's philosophy.

The venture began in 1903 as the George R. Rich Manufacturing Company of Chicago. Rich, a mechanic in the rolling mill of the Illinois Steel Company, had invented a unique type of high-speed industrial drill; his fledgling enterprise began manufacturing drills and reamers out of a tiny factory in a Chicago basement. Eugene Clark moved the facilities to Buchanan, Michigan, in 1904. Three years later it became the Celfor Tool Company. As its high-quality drills won fame, the firm expanded and diversified. In 1911 Celfor organized the Buchanan Electric Steel Company, built one of the first electric steel furnaces in America, and began producing fine castings of carbon and steel alloys. It pioneered in developing cast-steel disc wheels for motor trucks

to replace the traditional wooden-spoke wheels. In 1916 the business first produced a new close-drive type of axle and, on December 27 of that year, became the Clark Equipment Company.

World War I produced a tremendous demand for Clark's high-quality products and the firm manufactured axles and wheels by the thousands for military use. To facilitate moving the heavy axles and wheels around the shop, several employees invented a gas-powered, three-wheeled, materials-handling truck. Visiting customers liked the "tructractor" so well that they ordered some for their own use. As a result, in 1917 the Clark Tructractor division began production. By 1918, as Clark nationally advertised its tructractors, the thriving concern could hardly keep up with orders.

In 1920 Clark opened a modern new factory in Battle Creek to manufacture axles. It soon revamped the facility to handle the growing tructractor business. The year 1928 brought an important stimulus to Clark's growth when it introduced the first fork-lift truck, called a "duat." In 1933 Clark displayed its materials-handling machines at the Chicago Century of Progress Exposition, as well as a futuristic Clark autotram, a combination train and bus. Five years later Clark produced the first counterbalanced, sit-down rider lift truck, called the "carloader."

The vital needs for high-speed

materials handling in the defense industry during World War II produced a boom for Clark. From an output of 500 machines in 1939, the Battle Creek plant turned out 23,000 in 1943. Clark constructed more fork-lift trucks and industrial towing tractors during the war years than the entire industry had produced in all the preceding years. The Battle Creek factory proudly flew the coveted Army/Navy "E" Award pennant for production excellence during the war, and the firm was thrust into national leadership in the field.

By 1949, as the materials-handling industry mushroomed, Clark's volume was more than 20 times that of 1939. In 1952 annual sales reached $131 million. During the postwar era Clark manufactured such innovative products as the pul-pac attachment, hydraulic free lift uprights, carton clamp attachments, nested I-beam rails, canted roller uprights, three-wheel electric trucks, and narrow-aisle trucks. Clark also introduced a rental system allowing customers to utilize the best equipment without making a capital investment, and today the Clark Rental System is the largest lessor in the industry.

The early 1960s brought expansion into the emerging field of automated systems, and currently Clark's seven models of automatic-retrieval system provide a steady flow of parts, raw materials, and finished goods. With more than 80 years of experience, the Clark Equipment Company, the world-wide materials-handling industry leader, continues to develop new technologies to move, manage, and store materials more efficiently.

During World War I there was great demand for Clark's high-quality axles and wheels. Through the ingenuity of several employees, the forerunner of this 1929 tructractor was built for heavy materials handling.

POST DIVISION OF GENERAL FOODS CORPORATION

Charles William Post came to Battle Creek in 1891 as a 37-year-old invalid and parlayed a cereal-based coffee substitute into a multimillion-dollar empire and inspired the Battle Creek "cereal boom."

A little enterprise that began in 1895 in an old Greek-revival barn on an investment of $68.76 has become General Foods—the biggest U.S. based-company operating solely in the food business. The man who launched the firm was Charles William Post and his product was Postum, a cereal coffee substitute. Cereal beverages had been around for years, but Post produced an exceptionally tasty drink—and through his imaginative and daring advertising created a market beyond his competitors' wildest dreams. As Post's aptly phrased advertising slogans—"It Makes Red Blood," "There's a Reason," and "The Road to Wellville"—caught America's fancy, trainloads of Postum puffed out of Battle Creek for national distribution.

Post developed his second successful product in 1898, Grape-Nuts, so named because it tasted nutty and was thought to contain grape sugar. The following year he

founded the Battle Creek Paper Company (later the Container and Carton Division) to manufacture packaging for his crunchy cereal. By the turn of the century he was clearing a profit of nearly a million dollars a year. Post's success created a rush by other entrepreneurs to cash in on the cereal business. The Battle Creek "cereal boom" saw close to 80 companies formed to manufacture strange-sounding breakfast foods, but most soon dropped by the wayside.

The year 1901 saw the opening of the Post Tavern in downtown Battle Creek, one of the finest and best-known hotels in the Midwest. The following year Post platted an 80-acre tract of land south of the factory site into home sites that he offered at affordable prices to his employees. In 1904 Post constructed an English half-timbered clubhouse, which he furnished with fine antiques and artwork to house his Grandin Advertising Agency. That same year he marketed his third great success, Elijah's Manna, which he later renamed Post Toasties. Other products followed: Krinkle, a cornflake, in 1910, and Post Tavern Porridge and Instant Postum in 1912. When C.W. Post died in 1914, his original $68.76 investment had grown to $70 million. Ownership of the thriving Postum Cereal Company passed to his daughter, Marjorie Merriweather Post.

The Roaring '20s ushered in a new era of growth for the organization. In 1922 Postum Cereal Company stock was placed on the open market, and the following year an employee's stock-option plan allowed workers to benefit as the firm grew. The acquisition of the

Jell-O Company in 1925 began the tremendous expansion of the Postum Cereal Company. Igleheart Flour and Minute Tapioca followed in 1926; Franklin Baker Coconut, Walter Baker Chocolate, and Log Cabin Syrup in 1927; Maxwell House Coffee and Calumet Baking Powder in 1928; and Birds Eye, Diamond Crystal Salt, and Certo Corporation in 1929. The Postum Cereal Company became General Foods Corporation in 1929 to better reflect its diversification.

Today Battle Creek's Post plant manufactures 15 different cereals ranging from Alpha-Bits to Grape-Nuts and Instant Postum. GF's Carton and Container Division, a manufacturer of packaging materials, still shares the plant site.

The policy C.W. Post developed—to manufacture products of the highest possible quality, maintain sanitary, safe, and pleasant working conditions, and to pay a just return for honest service rendered—continues to produce success for the Battle Creek business he founded in 1895.

By 1905 the buildings of the Post Cereal Company overshadowed the structure where C.W. Post got his start. The old Italianate farmhouse, which Post dubbed La Vita Inn, was the site of his venture in operating a health reform institution.

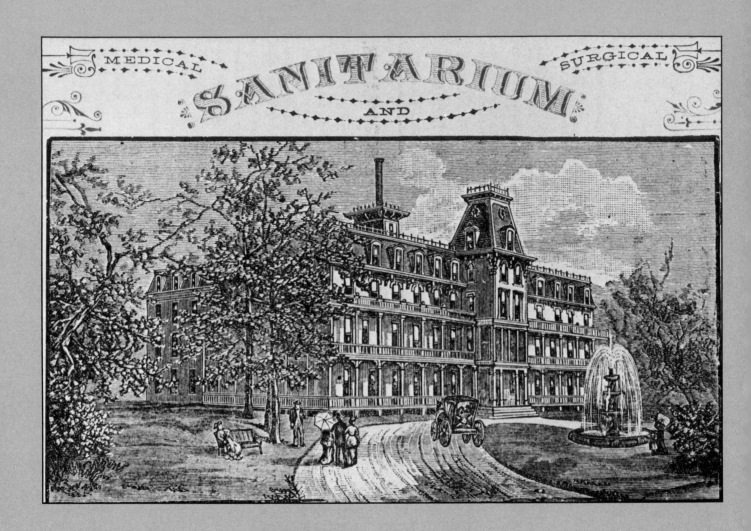

MEDICAL   SANITARIUM   SURGICAL

AND

Patrons

The following individuals, companies and organizations have made a valuable commitment to the quality of this publication. Windsor Publications and The Battle Creek Area Chamber of Commerce gratefully acknowledge their participation in *Battle Creek: The Place Behind the Products.*

Archway Cookies, Inc.*
Battle Creek Adventist Hospital*
Battle Creek Enquirer and The Miller Foundation*
Battle Creek Gas Company*
Battle Creek Schools*
Battle Creek Tent & Awning Co.
Beer Company of Battle Creek, Inc.
Clark Equipment Company*
Charles J. Crosby, D.O. Orthopedic Surgery
DeKorne Ethan Allen Galleries
Michael E. Downing, Associate Broker/Realtor RE/MAX Perrett Associates, Inc.
Elephant Ear Restaurant
Federal Home Companies*
Felpausch Food Centers*
Mrs. Oscar Holcomb Flanders
Greater Battle Creek Foundation
Jim Hazel's Union 76*
Hi-Lex Corporation*
HMO WEST, INC.
Isringhausen, Inc.*
Kellogg Company*
W.K. Kellogg Foundation*
Lakeview General Hospital/ Osteopathic*
Lakeview Square*
Lawson Printers, Inc./Columbia Graphics Ltd.
Eugene H. McKay, Jr.

Massachusetts Mutual Life Insurance Company*
Michigan Carton Corporation
Michigan National Bank*
Mickey's Newstand
Nippondenso Sales, Inc.*
Officeways, Inc.
Post Division of General Foods Corporation*
Professional Personnel Leasing, Inc.
A. Ratti and Sons*
R.W. Snyder Company, Inc.*
Joyce and Duff Stoltz
Stouffer Hotel*
John ter Avest Agency Inc.*
Junior & Frances Thornton
UNION ELECTRIC INC.
UNION PUMP COMPANY
Vandervoort, Cooke, McFee, Christ, Carpenter & Fisher, P.C., Attorneys
Worgess Insurance Agency

*Partners in Progress of *Battle Creek: The Place Behind the Products.* The histories of these companies and organizations appear in Chapter 7, beginning on page 97.

Facing page: *By the 1880s Battle Creek could be justly proud of its innovative health care facilities. This drawing of the Sanitarium appeared in an 1886 state gazetteer. Courtesy, Western Michigan University Archives*

Bibliography

Andrews, J.N. *History of the Sabbath. . . .* Battle Creek: Seventh-Day Adventist Publishing Association, 1862.

Art Souvenir Edition of the Battle Creek Daily Moon. Battle Creek: [1900].

Barrett, J.O. *The Spiritual Pilgrim: a Biography of James M. Peebles.* Boston: William White & Company, 1871.

Bates, Joseph. *Autobiography of Joseph Bates.* Battle Creek: Seventh-Day Adventist Publishing Association, 1868.

The Battle Creek Idea. Vol. 28, No. 1. Summer, 1928.

Battle Creek Sesquicentennial Committee. *Battle Creek 150: Sesquicentennial, 1831-1981.* Battle Creek, 1980.

Beers, F.W. *Atlas of Calhoun County, Michigan.* New York: F.W. Beers & Co., 1873.

Bingay, Malcolm S. *Of Me I Sing.* Indianapolis: Bobbs-Merrill Company, [1949].

Bryce, J.W. *Random Rhymes.* Battle Creek: [Ellis Publishing Co.], 1899.

Burr, C.B., editor. *Medical History of Michigan.* 2 vols. Minneapolis: Bruce Publishing Company, 1930.

Cadwallader, M.E. *Hydesville in History.* Chicago: the Progressive Thinker Publishing House, 1922.

Calhoun County Circuit Court Records. In Western Michigan University Archives and Regional History Collections.

Cannon, C.S. *Universal Proof of Money Making . . .* Battle Creek: C.S. Canon & Co., 1880.

Canright, D.M. *Seventh-Day Adventism Renounced. . . .* Kalamazoo: Kalamazoo Publishing Co., 1888.

Carson, Gerald. *Cornflake Crusade.* New York: Rinehart and Company, [1957].

Catalogue, Dr. Peebles' Pamphlets and Books. n.p. n.d.

[Chase, Warren]. *The Life-Line of the Lone One. . . .* 2nd ed. Boston: Bela March, 1858.

"The City of Battle Creek—Its Early History, Growth, and Present Condition." *Report of the Pioneer Society of the State of Michigan.* Vol. 3, 1881.

Coller, Ross H. *Battle Creek's Centennial, 1859-1959.* Battle Creek: Battle Creek Enquirer and News, 1959.

Committee on Publicity. *Battle Creek Centennial, 1831-1931.* Battle Creek: Ellis Publishing Company, 1931.

Daniels, W.H., ed. *The Temperance Reform and Its Great Reformers. . . .* New York: Nelson & Phillips, 1878.

Doutney, Thomas N. *His Life-Struggle, Fall, and Reformation. . . .* Battle Creek: William C. Gage & Sons, 1891.

Drs. Peebles and Burroughs: Specialists. Battle Creek, [1900].

[Durant, Samuel W.]. *History of Kalamazoo County, Michigan. . . .* Philadelphia: Everts and Abbott, 1880.

Earl, Stephen Van Rensselaer. "Earl Diaries." Bound photocopies of manuscript diaries, 19 vols. 1860-1885. In Western Michigan University Archives and Regional History Collections.

Fairfield, W.J. *The Man that Rum Made.* Battle Creek: J.E. White Publishing Company, [1886].

Fauset, Arthur Huff. *Sojourner Truth: God's Faithful Pilgrim.* Chapel Hill: University of North Carolina Press, 1938.

Fifty Years at Post Products. Battle Creek, 1945.

Gardner, Washington. *History of Calhoun County Michigan.* Chicago: Lewis Publishing Company, 1913. 2 vols.

[Gilbert, Olive]. *Narrative of Sojourner Truth. . . .* Boston, 1875.

Good Health. Vol. 46, 1911; 47, 1912; 61, 1926.

Hardinage, Emma. *Modern American Spiritualism . . .* New York, 1870.

The Health Reformer. Vol. 3, 1868-1869. Battle Creek.

Hill, W.B. *Experiences of a Pioneer Minister of Minnesota.* Minneapolis: J.A. Folsom, 1892.

History of Calhoun County, Michigan. Philadelphia: L.H. Everts, 1877.

Johnson, A.S. *A Treatise on Nervous, Chronic, and Special Diseases. . . .* Battle Creek, [1879].

Kellogg, John H. *Autointoxication by Intestinal Toxemia.* Battle Creek: Modern Medicine Publishing Co., 1919.

_____ . *Dr. Kellogg's Lectures on Practical Health Topics. Vol. 2, The Monster Malady. . . .* Battle Creek: Good Health Publishing Co., 1913.

_____ . *Dyspepsia, Its Causes, Prevention and Cure.* Battle Creek: Good Health Publishing Company, 1879.

_____ . *A Household Manual. . . .* Battle Creek: Health Reformer, 1877.

_____ . *The Household Monitor of Health.* Battle Creek: Good Health Publishing Company, 1891.

_____ . *The Itinerary of a Breakfast.* Revised ed. New York: Funk & Wagnalls Company, 1926.

_____ . *Ladies' Guide in Health and Disease.* Battle Creek: Modern Medicine Publishing Co., 1898.

_____ . *Plain Facts for Old and Young. . . .* New ed. Burlington, Iowa: I.F. Segner & Co., 1890.

[_____] . *Sunbeams of Health and Temperance.* Battle Creek: Health Publishing Company, 1887.

Kellogg, M.G. *The Bath: Its Use and Application.* Battle Creek: The Health Reformer, 1873.

Loughborough, J.N. *The Great Second Advent Movement. . . .* Nashville, Tennessee: Southern Publishing Association, [1905].

Lowe, Berenice Bryant. *Tales of Battle Creek.* Battle Creek, 1976.

Maxson, J.D. *Guide to Health. . . .* Albion: Mirror Office, 1862.

Michigan Bureau of Labor and Industrial Statistics. *Annual Reports.*

Lansing, 1884-1920. Title varies.

Nostrums and Quackery. 2nd ed. Chicago: American Medical Association Press, 1912.

Nostrums and Quackery. Vol. 2. Chicago: American Medical Association Press, 1921.

Peebles, J.M. *Seers of the Ages.* . . . Chicago: Progressive Thinker Publishing House, 1903.

Pioneer und Historical Society Collections. Report of the Pioneer Society of the State of Michigan Together With Reports of County, Town, and District Pioneer Societies. Lansing: W.S. George & Company, 1877-1929. 40 vols. Also 2 vol. index.

Polk, R.L. *Michigan State Gazetteer and Business Directory.* Detroit: R.L. Polk, 1885; 1895-1896; 1911; 1917-1918; 1931-1932.

Portrait and Biographical Album of Calhoun County . . . Chicago: Chapman Brothers, 1891.

Powell, Horace B. *The Original Has This Signature—W.K. Kellogg.* Englewood Cliffs, N.J.: Prentice-Hall, [1956].

The Road to Wellville. Battle Creek: Postum Cereal Co., n.d.

Roberts, E.W. *Pioneer Days in Old Battle Creek: an Illustrated and Descriptive Atlas of a City in the Making.* Battle Creek: Central Bank and Trust, 1931.

Rupp, I. Daniel. *An Original History of the Religious Denominations.* . . . Philadelphia: J.Y. Humphreys, 1844.

Rust, E.G. *Calhoun County Business Directory for 1869-70 . . . with a Detailed History of the County.* . . . Battle Creek, 1869.

Schaefer, Richard A. *Legacy.* . . . Mountain View, California: Pacific Press Association, [1977].

Schwarz, Richard A. *John Harvey Kellogg, M.D.* Nashville, Tennessee: Southern Publication Association, 1970.

Seventy-Fifth Anniversary of General Foods Corporation, Post Division. . . . Supplement to the *Battle Creek Enquirer and News,* January 11, 1970.

Smith, Uriah. *Daniel and the Revelation.* Battle Creek: Review and Herald Publishing Company, 1897.

———. *Our Country: Its Past, Present, and Future.* . . . Battle Creek: Review and Herald, 1886.

Street, Julian. *Abroad at home.* . . . New York: the Century Company, 1914.

A Summer at the Post Tavern. n.p. n.d.

"There's a Reason." Battle Creek: Gage Printing Co., [ca. 1915].

United States Bureau of the Census. Manuscript Products of Agriculture and Products of Industry Special Schedules, Calhoun County, 1850-1870.

United States Bureau of the Census. Manuscript Federal Population Census, Calhoun County, 1840-1910.

United States Department of the Treasury. Internal Revenue Assessment Lists. Michigan, 1862-1866.

Van Buren, Anson DePuy. "History of the Churches in Battle Creek." *Report of the Pioneer Society of the State of Michigan.* Vol. 5 (1884).

Waggoner, J.H. *The Nature and Tendency of Modern Spiritualism.* Battle Creek: Review and Herald, 1860.

White, Ellen G. *The Health Reform and the Health Institute.* Battle Creek: Seventh-Day Adventist Publishing Association, 1872.

White, James. *Sketches of the Christian Life and Public Labors of William Miller.* Battle Creek: Seventh-Day Adventist Publishing Association, 1875.

White, James Edson. *The Coming King.* Battle Creek: Review and Herald, 1900.

White, J.E. & Parsons, W.F. *Parsons' Hand-Book of Forms.* . . . Battle Creek: J.E. White, 1882.

Whiting, R. Augusta. *A Biography of A.B. Whiting.* . . . Boston: William White and Company, 1872.

W.K. Kellogg Foundation: the First Half-Century, 1930-1980. n.p. n.d.

Manuscript Sources.

Among the manuscript collections in the Willard Library, the following proved very helpful: the Ross H. Coller collection of file cards; the vertical file; the Art Middleton clipping collection entitled, "This Was Battle Creek;" E.W. Roberts' notebooks titled "Rambles With a Camera Around Old Battle Creek;" and Michael Gregory's typescript chronicle of important dates. The Willard Library collection of newspapers on microfilm and photograph files were equally important.

The Western Michigan University Archives and Regional History Collections houses a wide variety of public documents with information on Calhoun County. Manuscript census returns and special census schedules gave much insight, as did the "Civil War Income Tax Rolls" for the county. In addition, the Archives holds the property tax assessment rolls for Calhoun County and the Calhoun County Circuit Court case files.

Acknowledgments

The authors would like to recognize the variety of individuals whose help made this book possible. Mr. Mike Smalla, Director of the Willard Public Library, Marlene Steele, and Jane Ratner extended every courtesy and opened the files of their marvelous local history collection. The Western Michigan University Archives and Regional History Collections made available an extensive collection of Calhoun County records. Mr. Duff Stoltz, curator of the Adventist Hospital Museum, gave us advice and access to much material, as did both the Kellogg and Post companies. Louise Rich and Mary Mitchell provided editorial assistance, while Opal Ellis, Sylvania Remeta, and Judith Massie typed tirelessly. Kanti Sandhu provided expert help copying and providing photographs.

Four hundred male employees of the Kellogg Company, dressed in immaculate white work uniforms paraded down Battle Creek's Main Street, now Michigan Avenue, on July 4, 1911. Copyright, 1984, courtesy, Kellogg Company

Index

THIS BOOK IS SET IN
PONTIAC AND LUBALIN TYPES,
PRINTED ON
70-POUND ACID-FREE MEAD OFFSET ENAMEL
AND BOUND BY
WALSWORTH PUBLISHING COMPANY